Irina Vinnik

Magic Scope
Coloring Book

112 designs & motifs

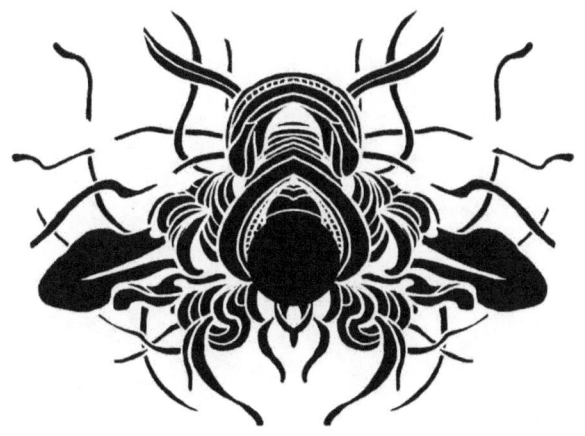

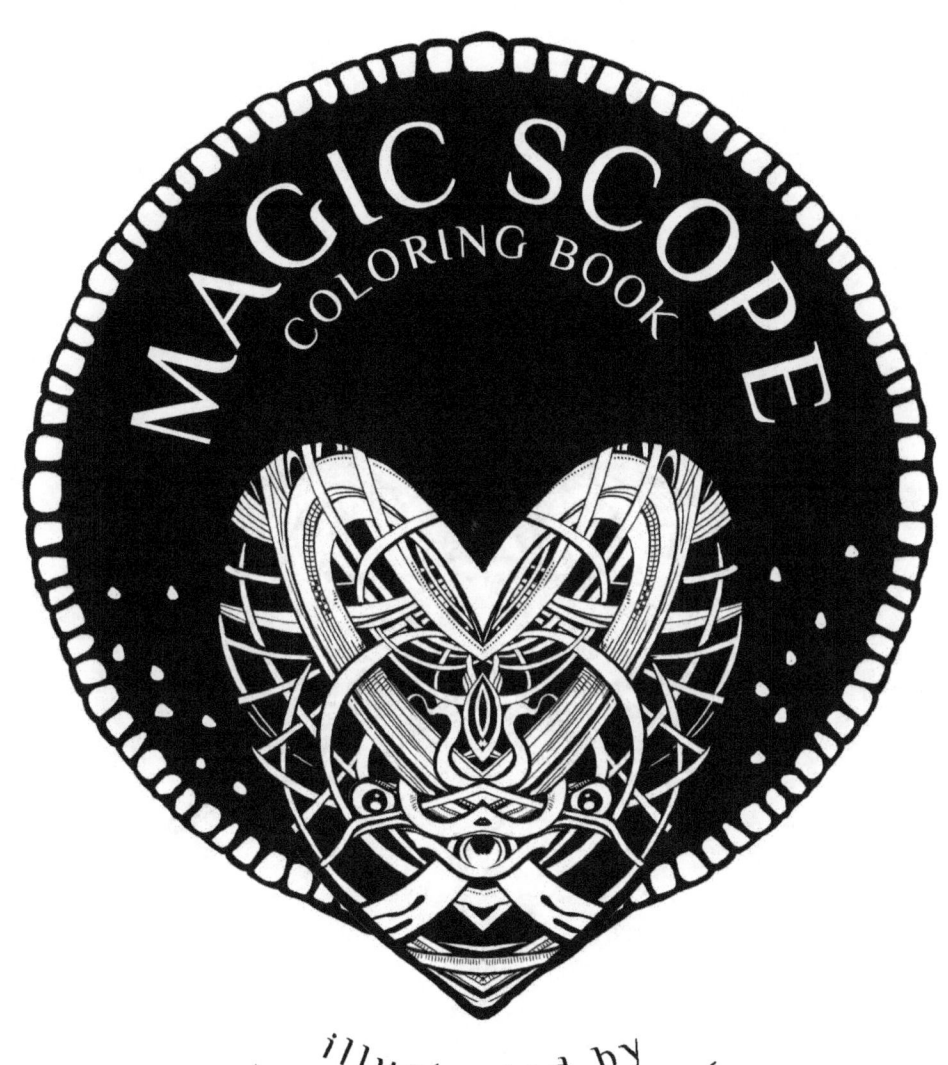

MAGIC SCOPE
COLORING BOOK

illustrated by
IRINA VINNIK

2016

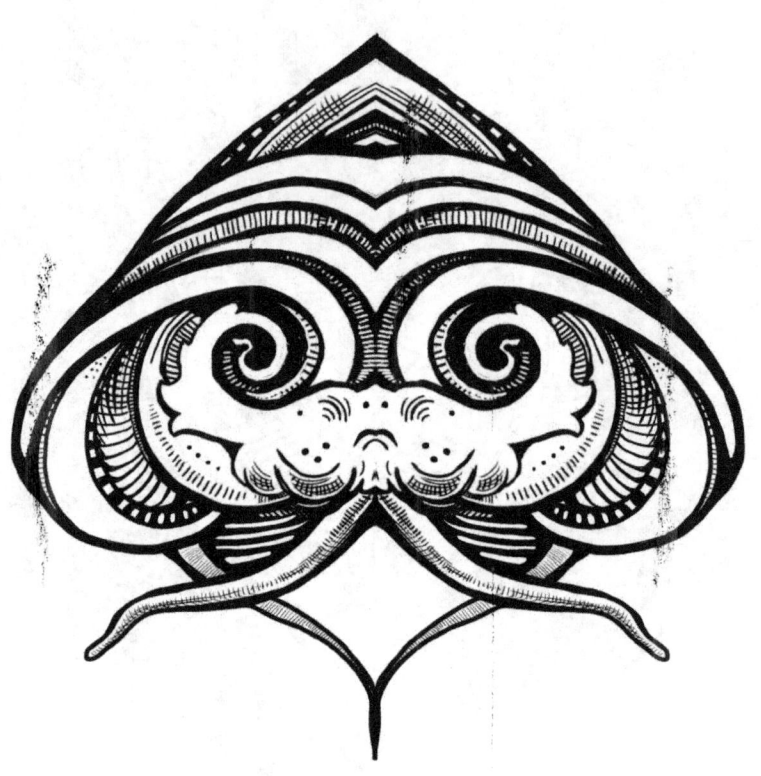

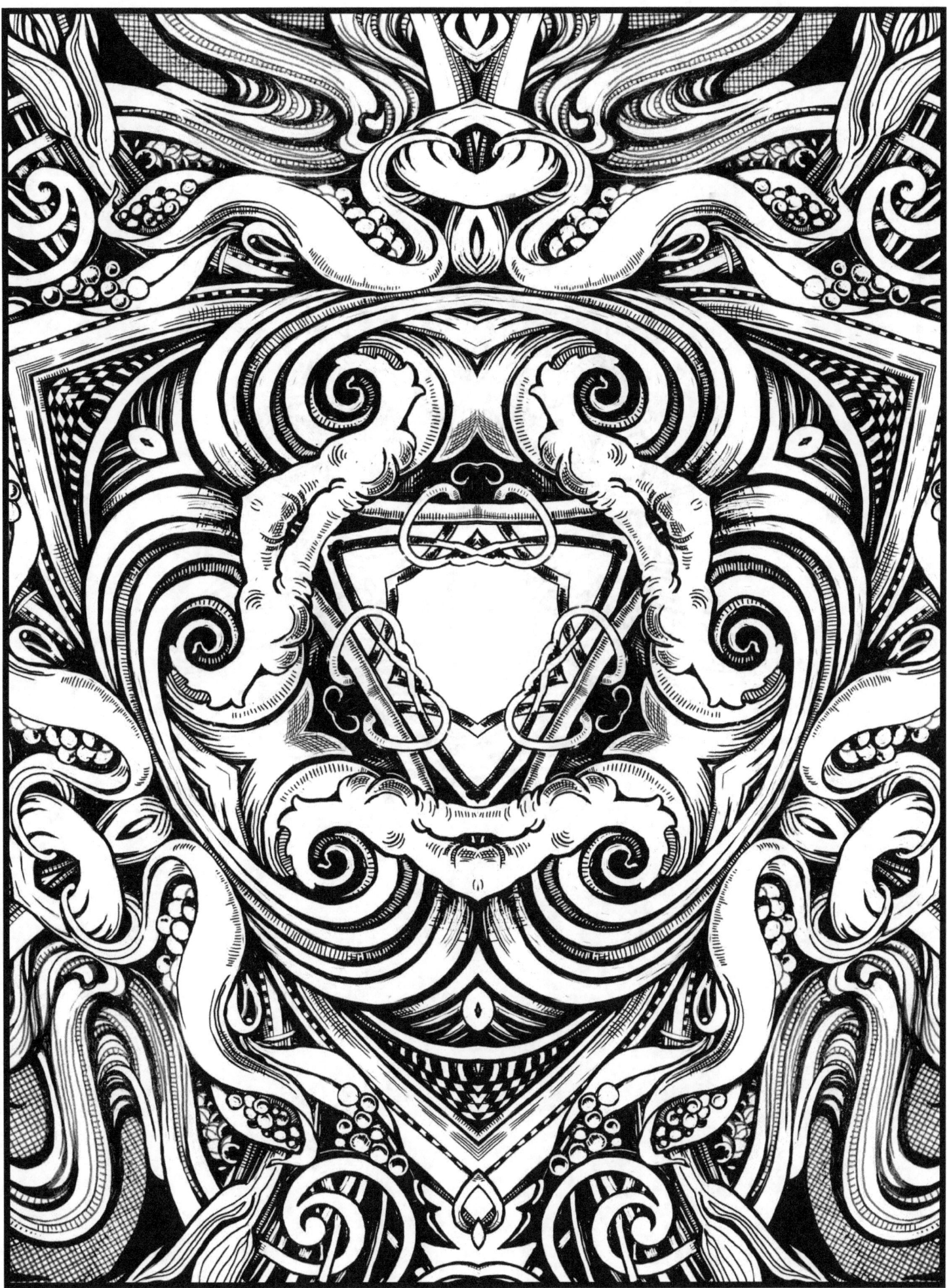

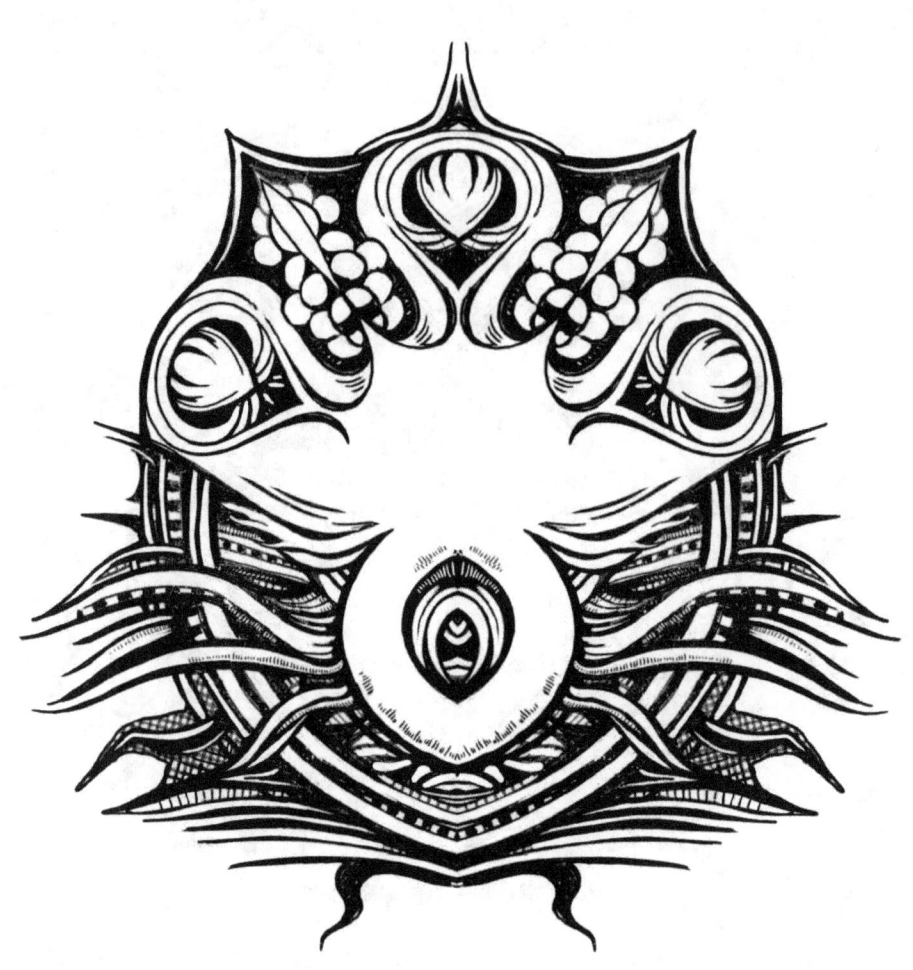

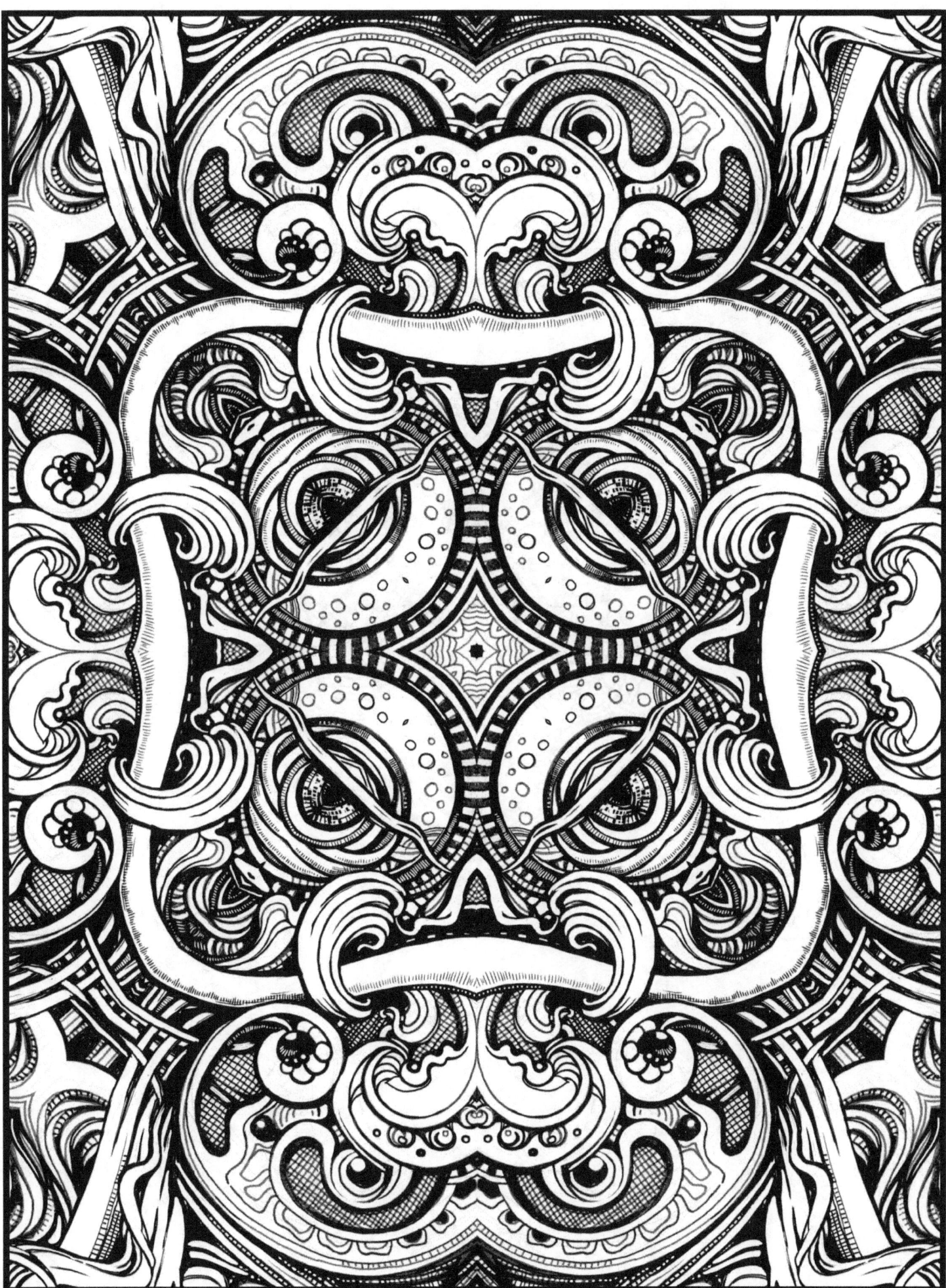

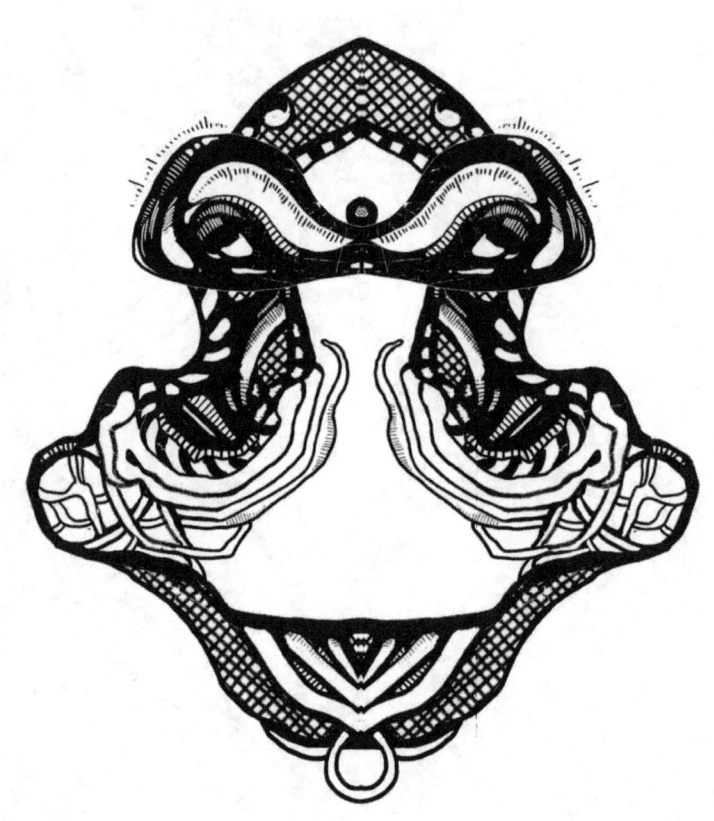

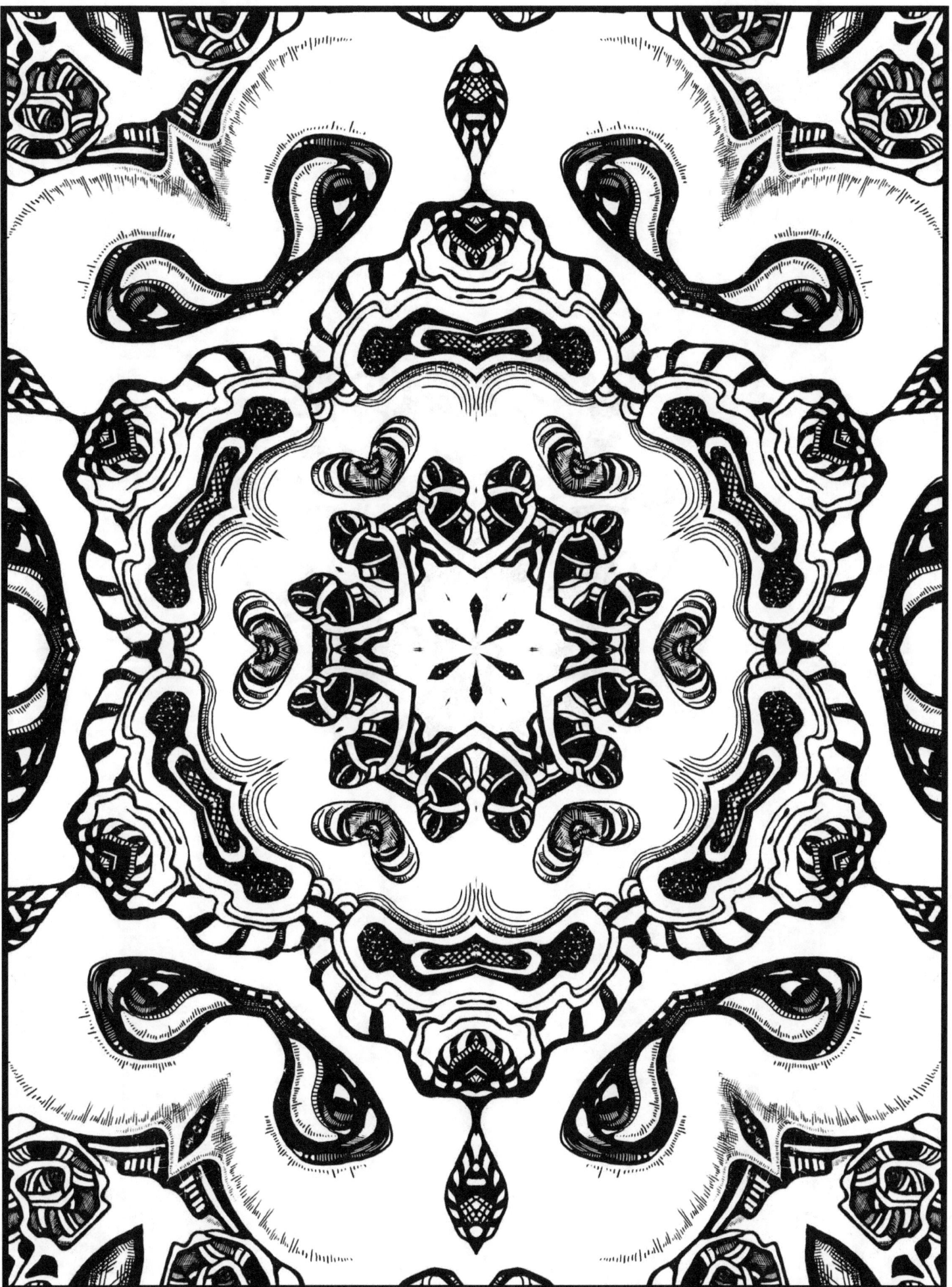

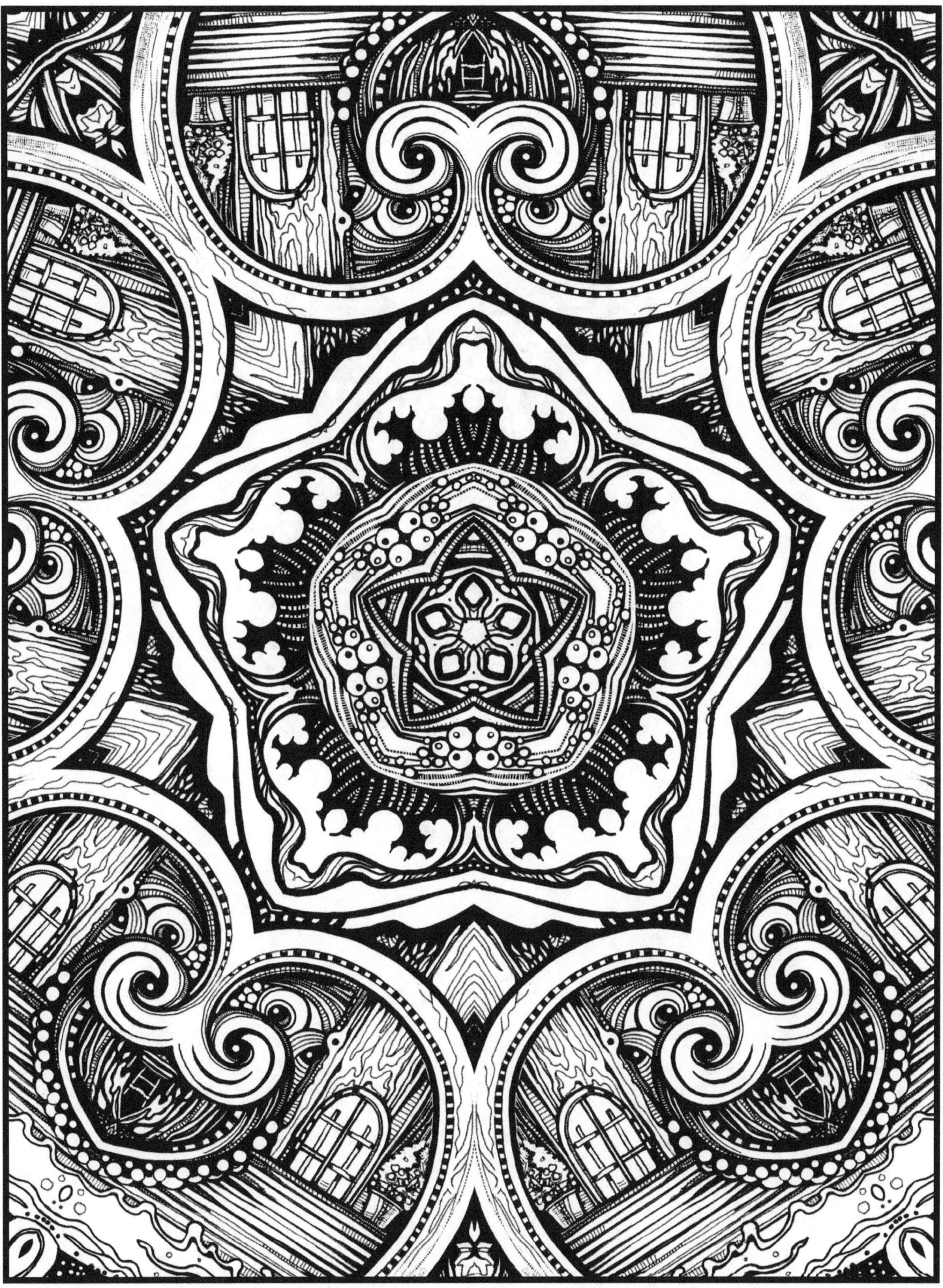

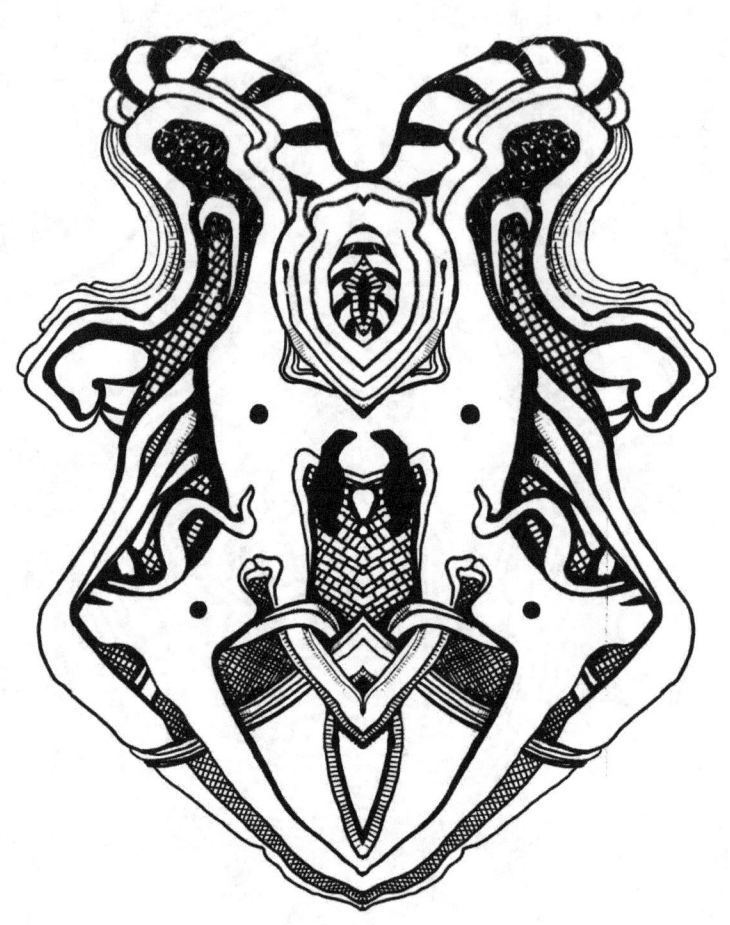

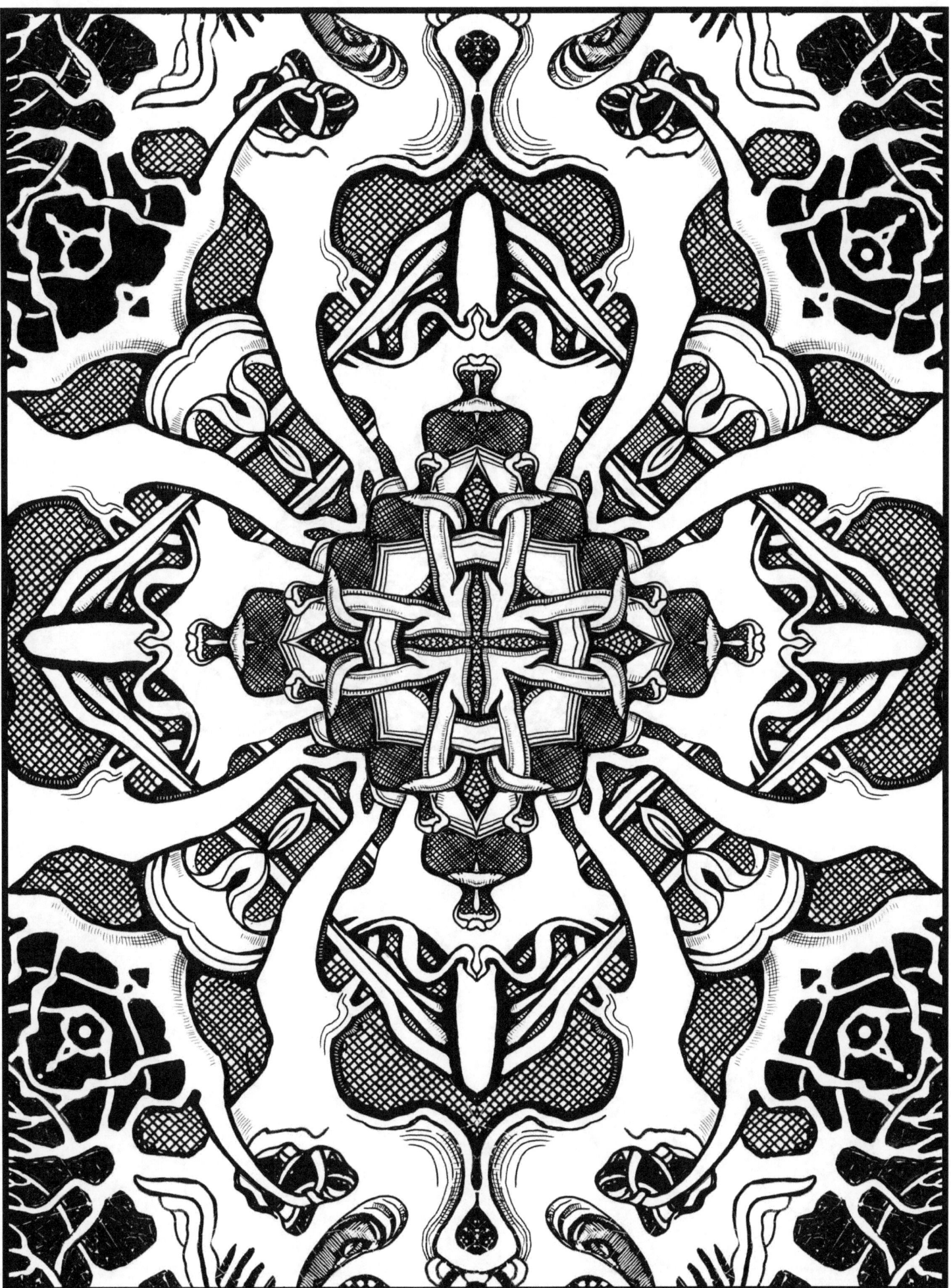

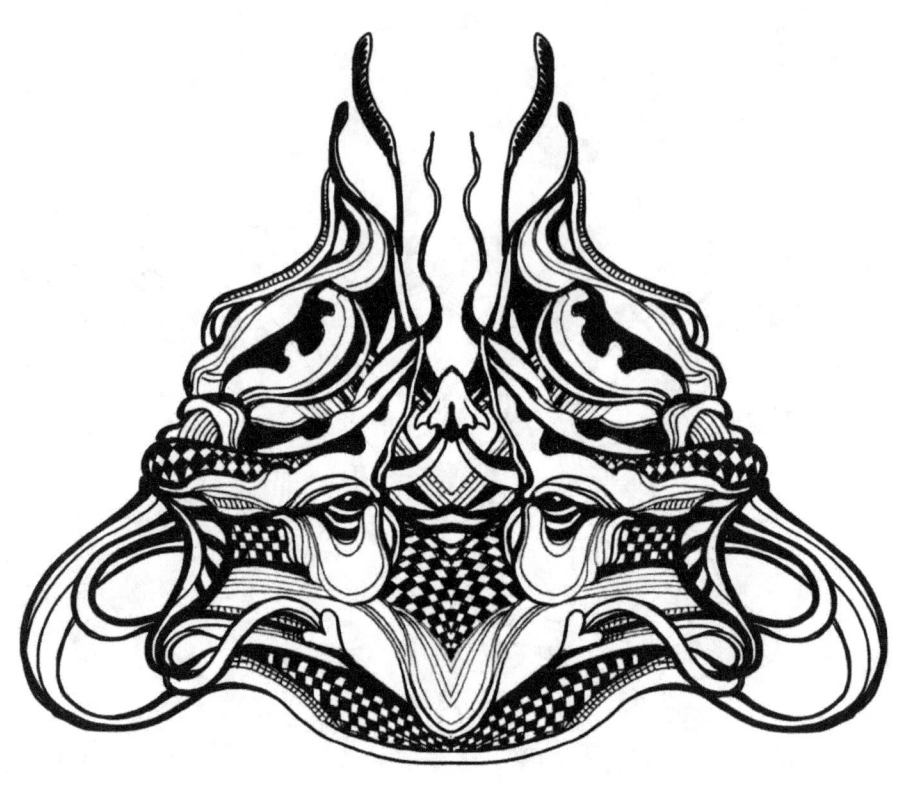

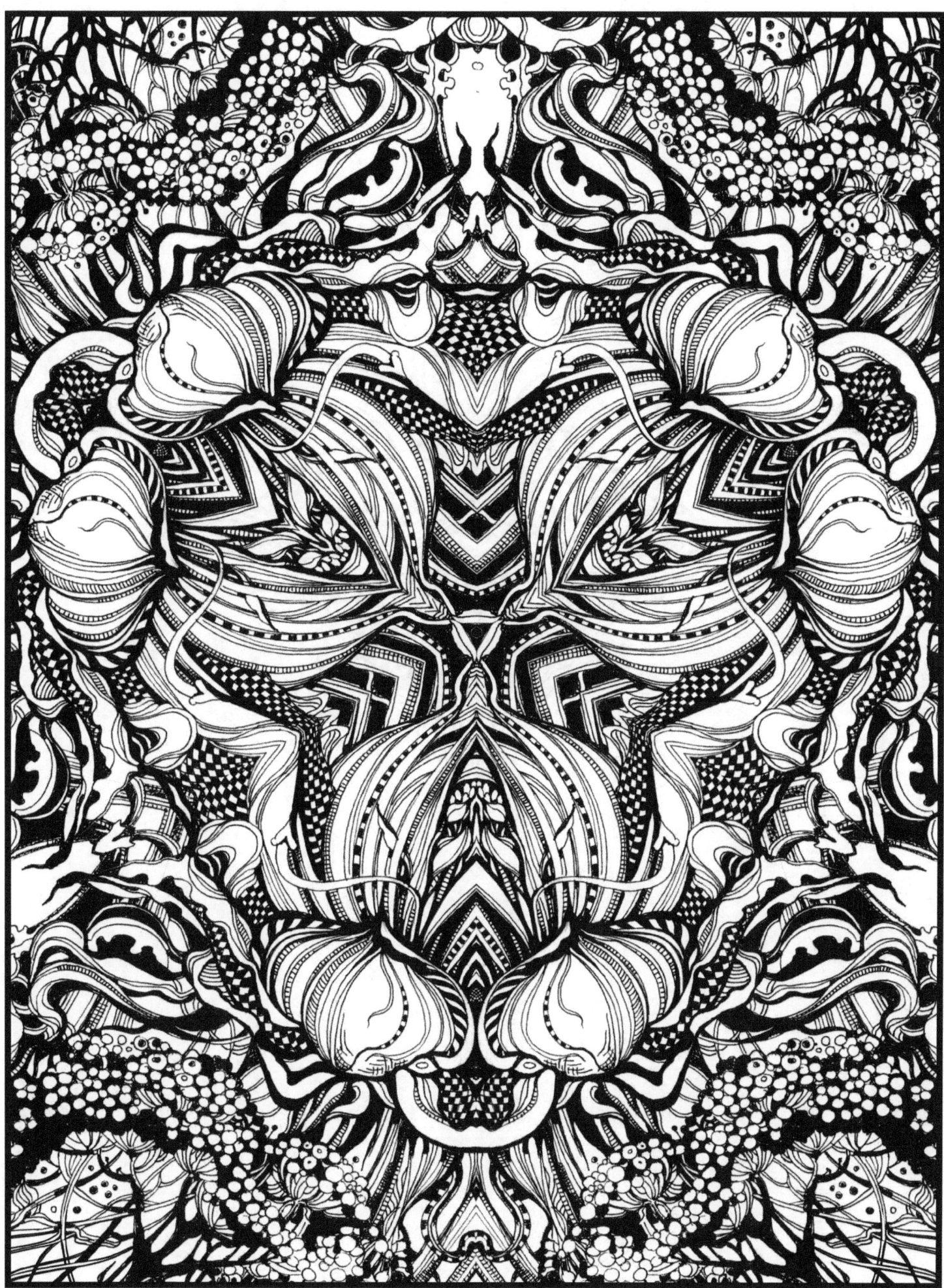

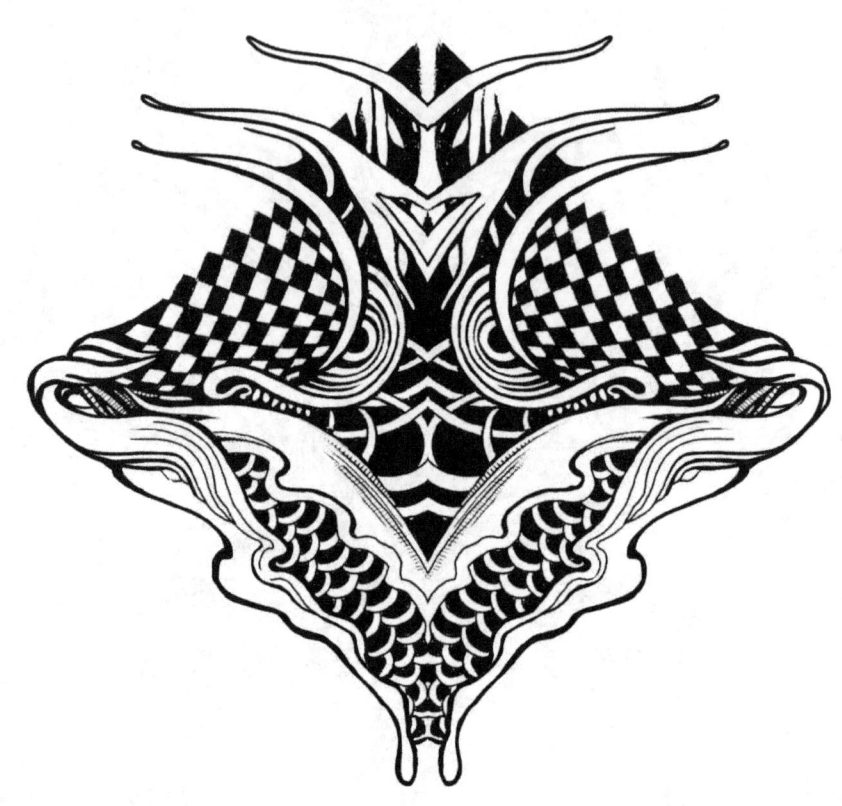

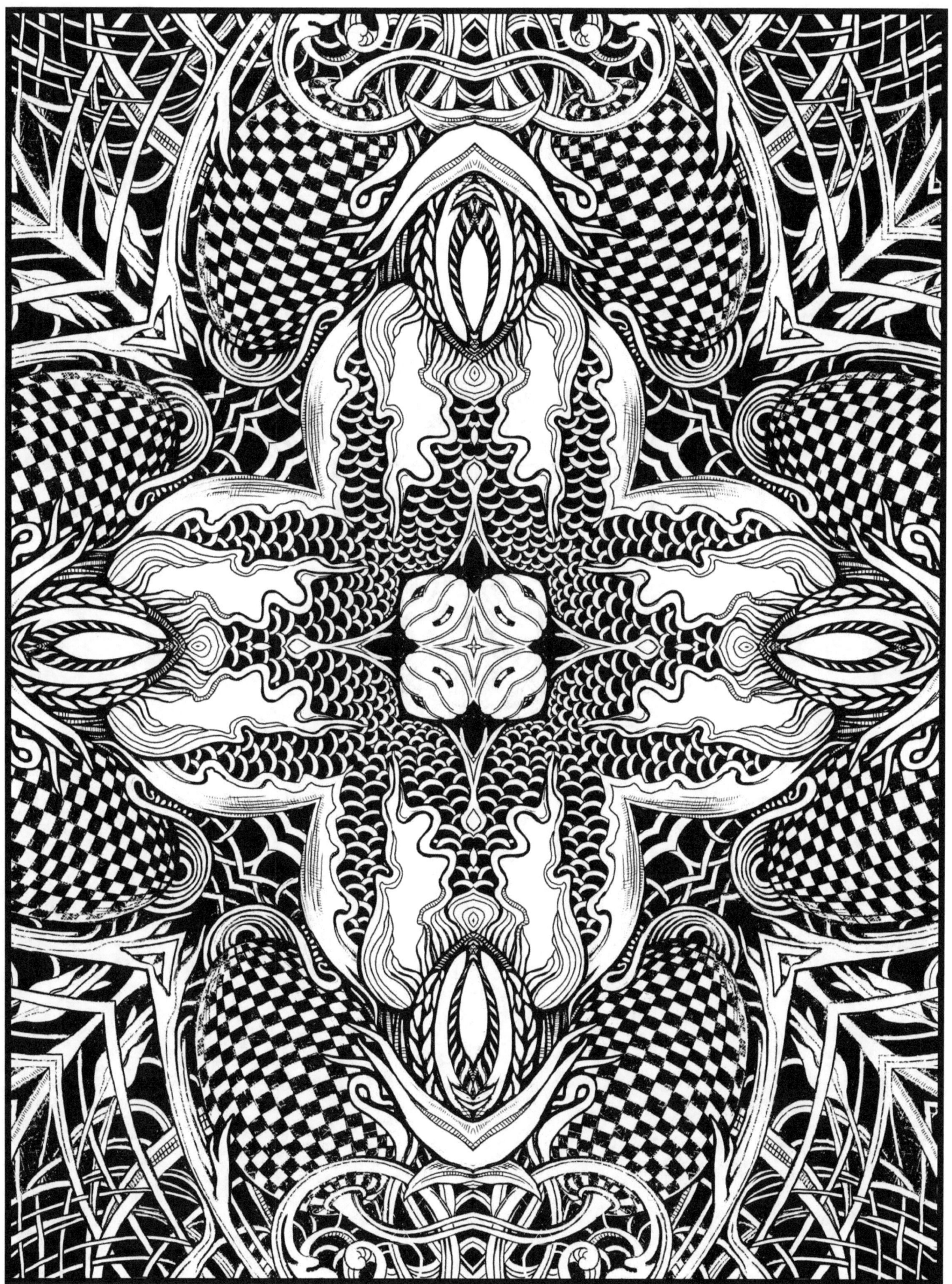

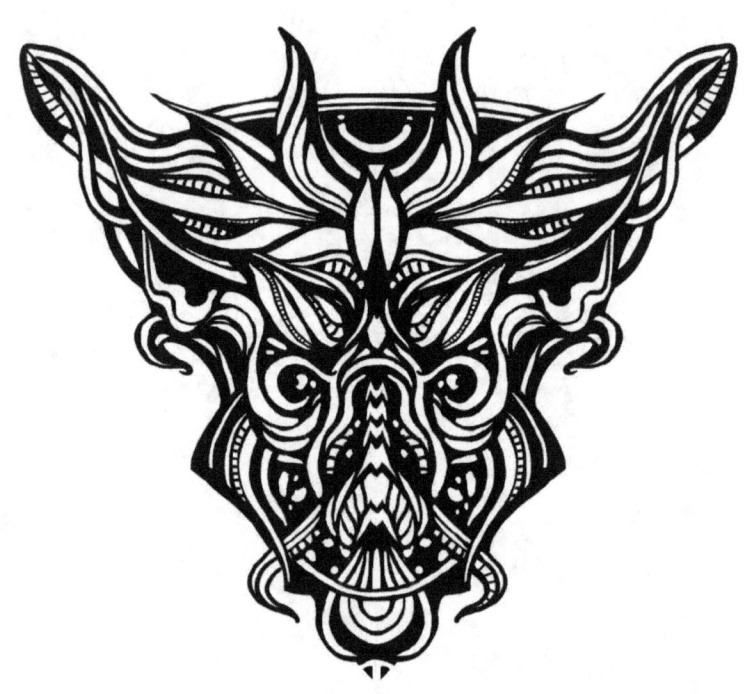

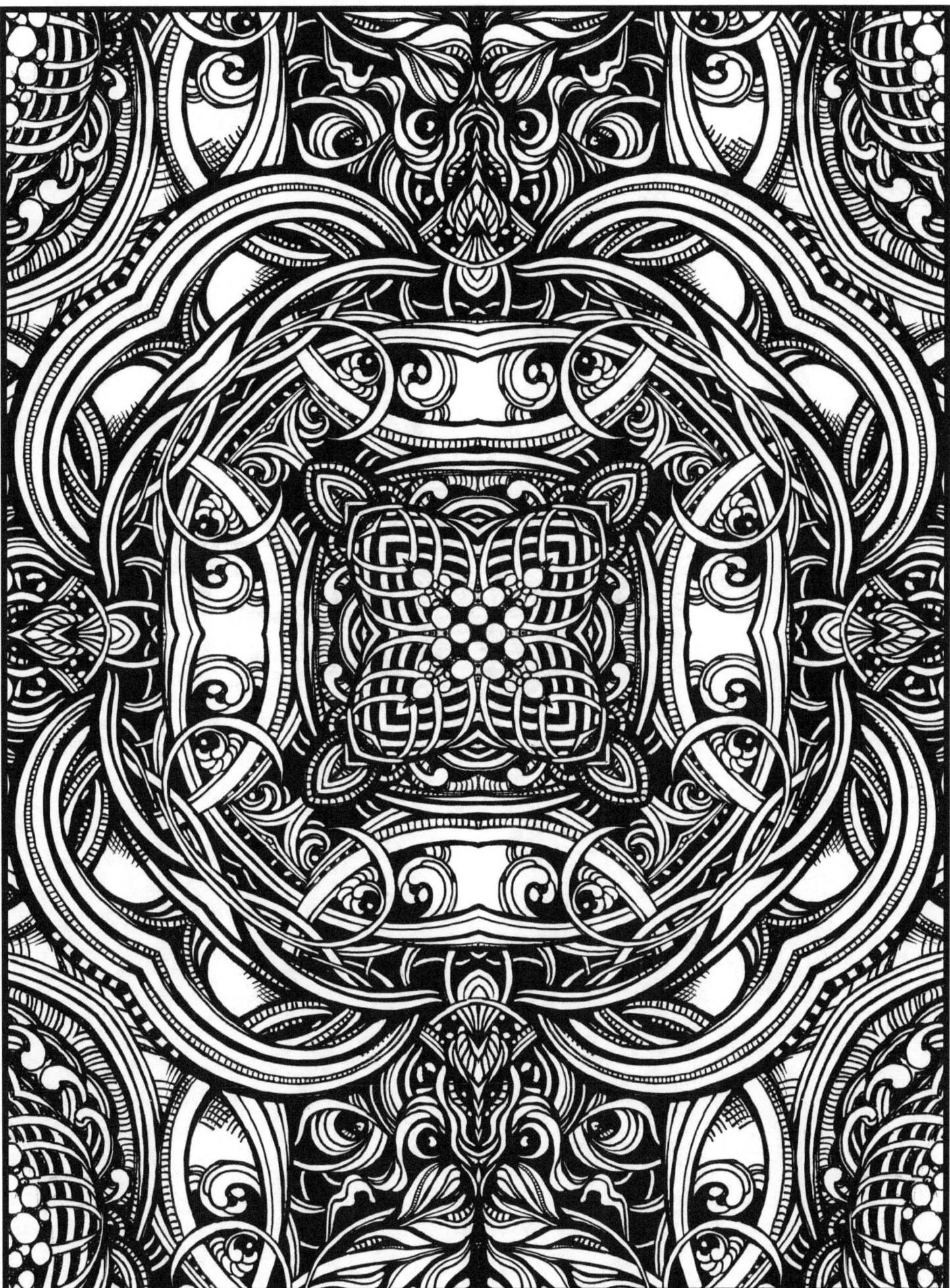

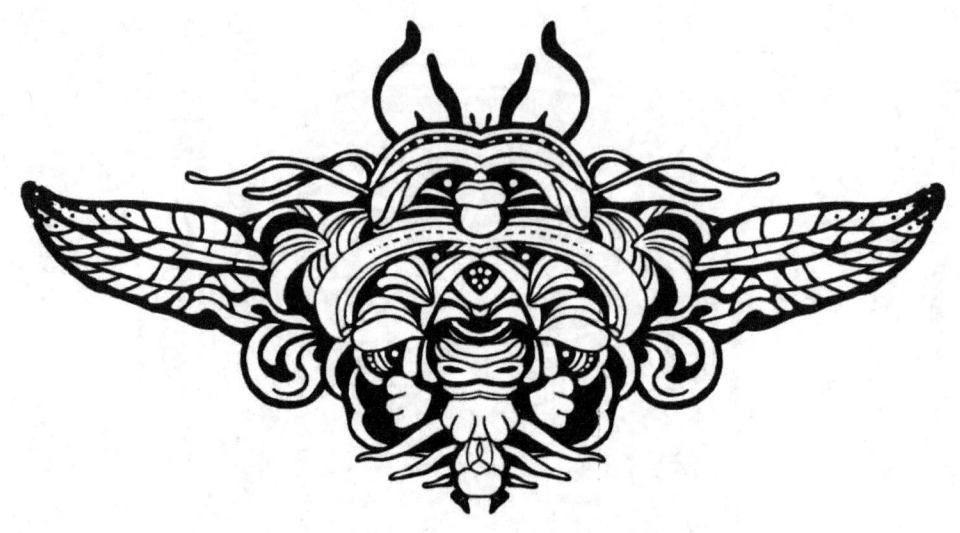

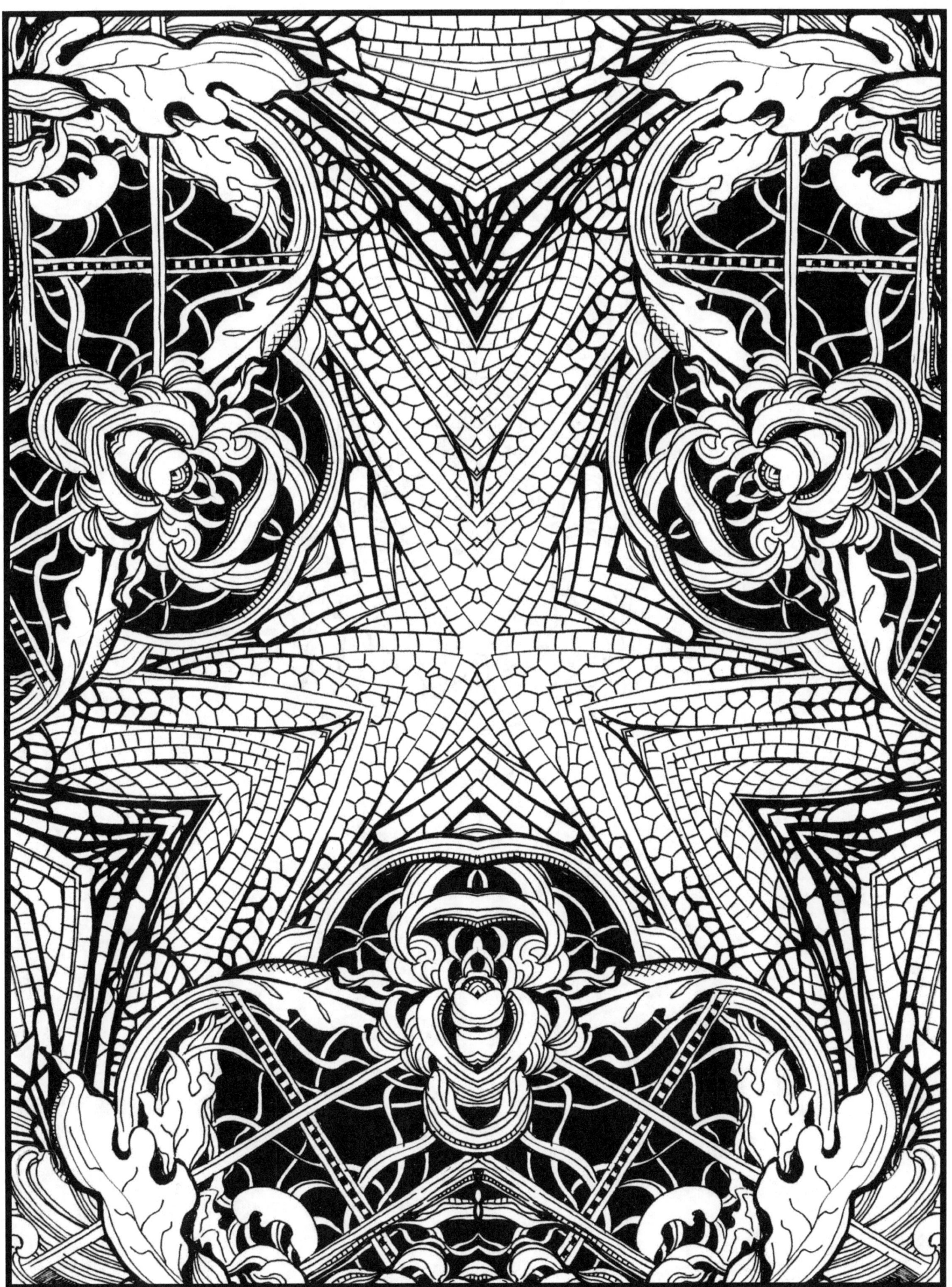

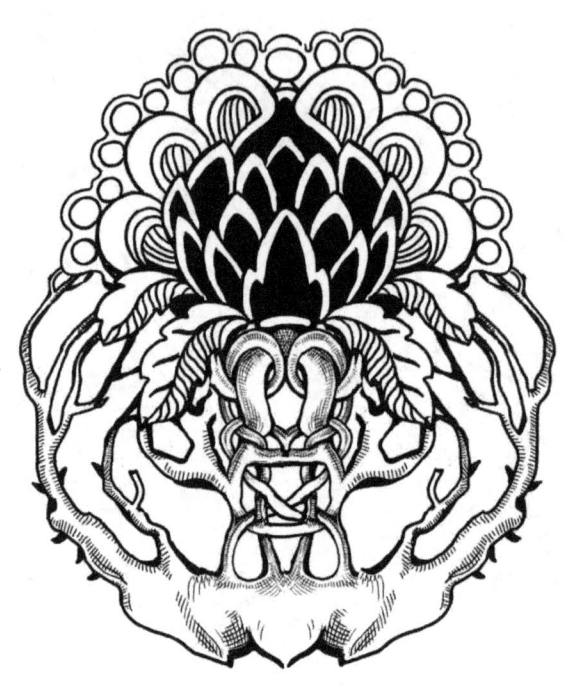

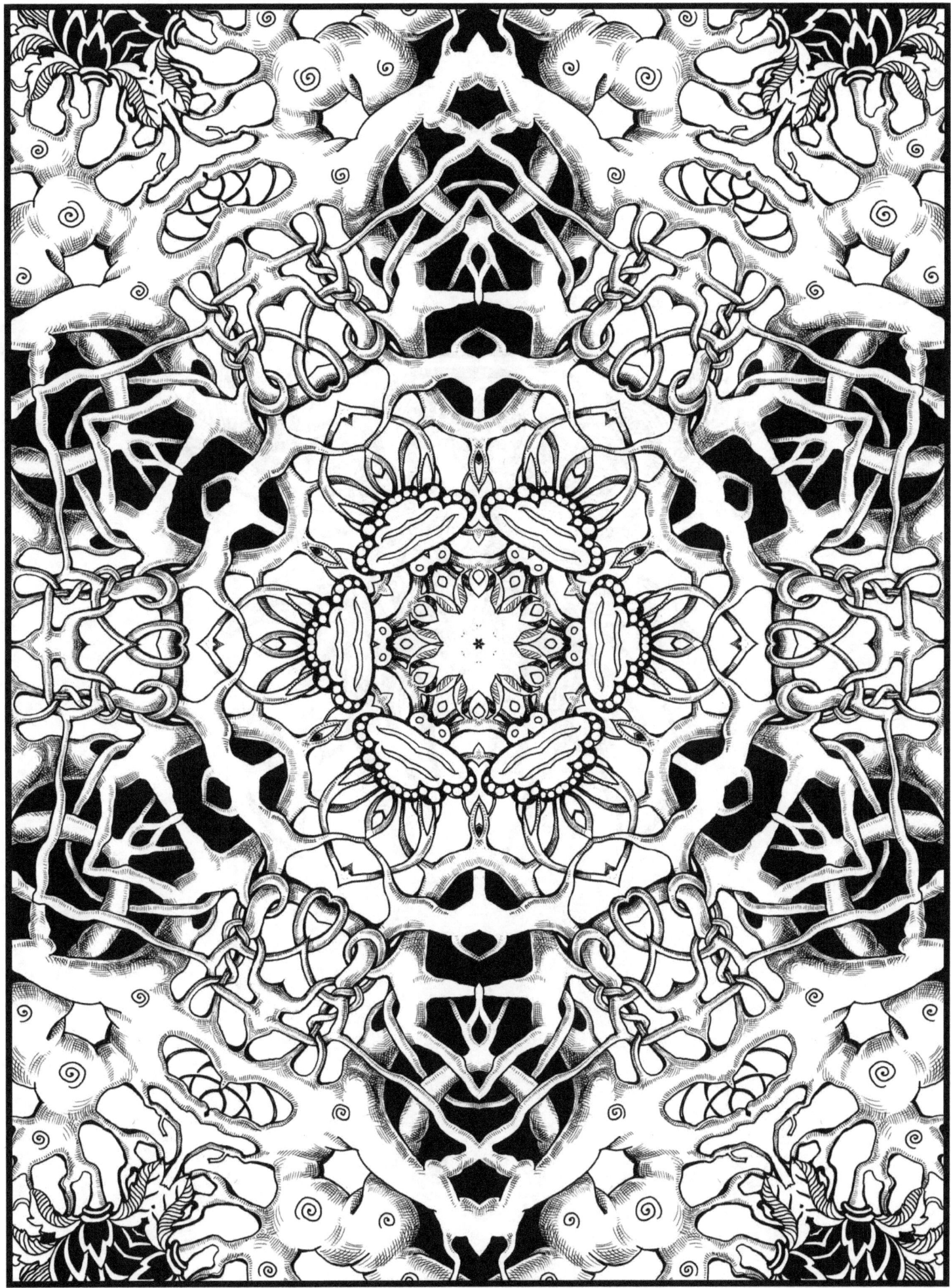

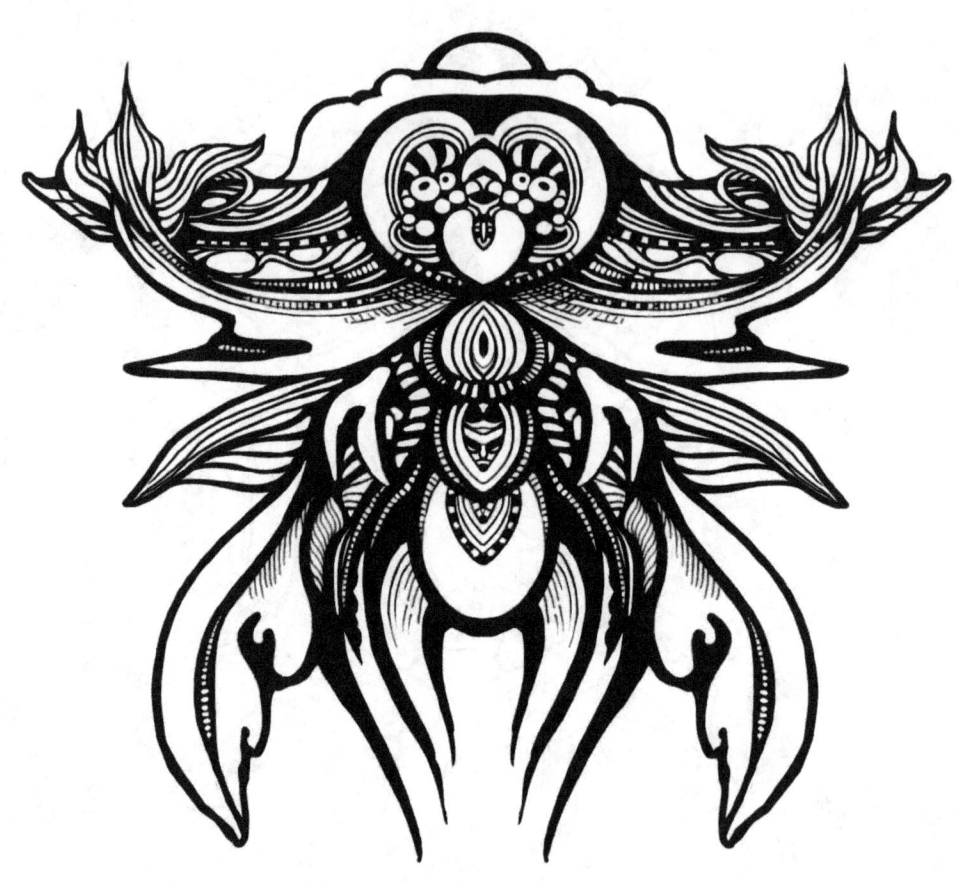

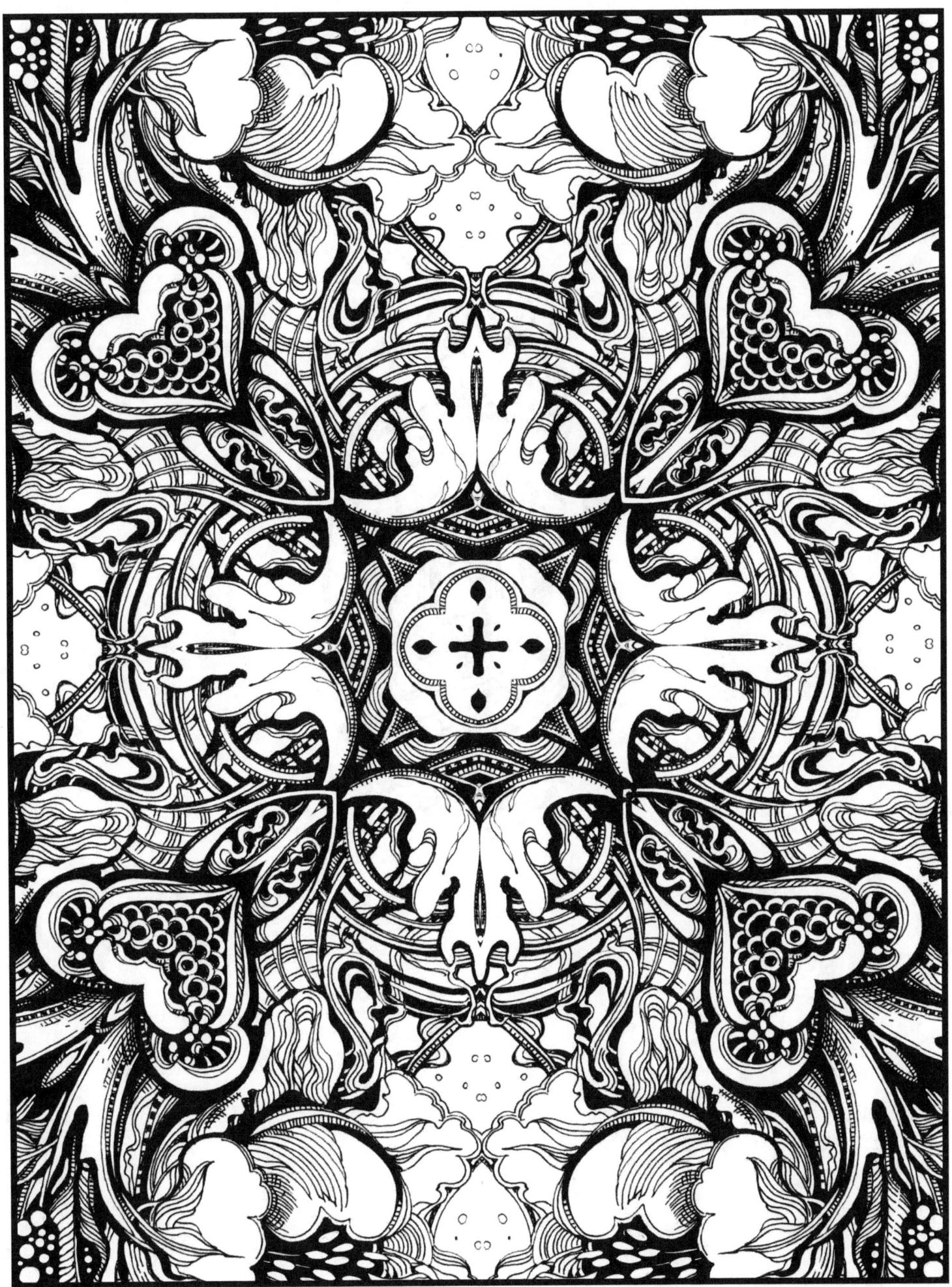

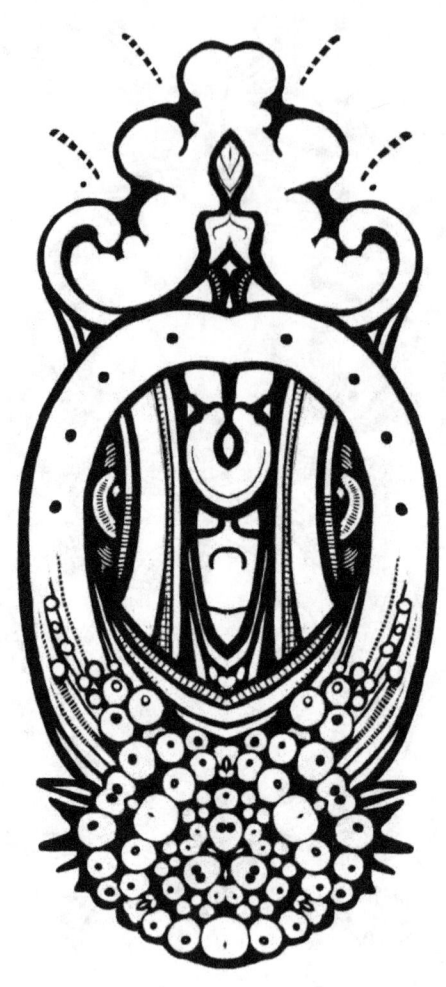

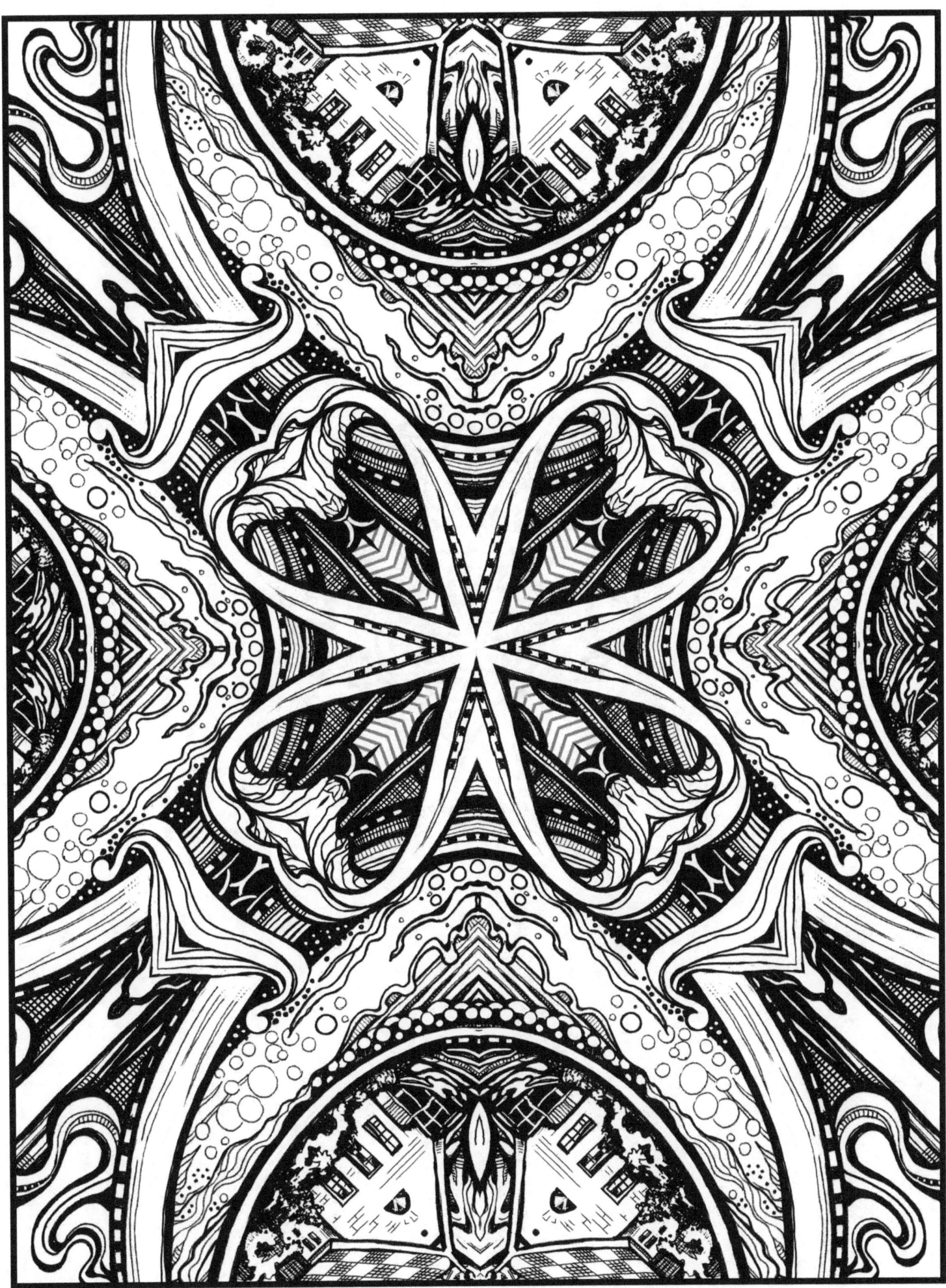

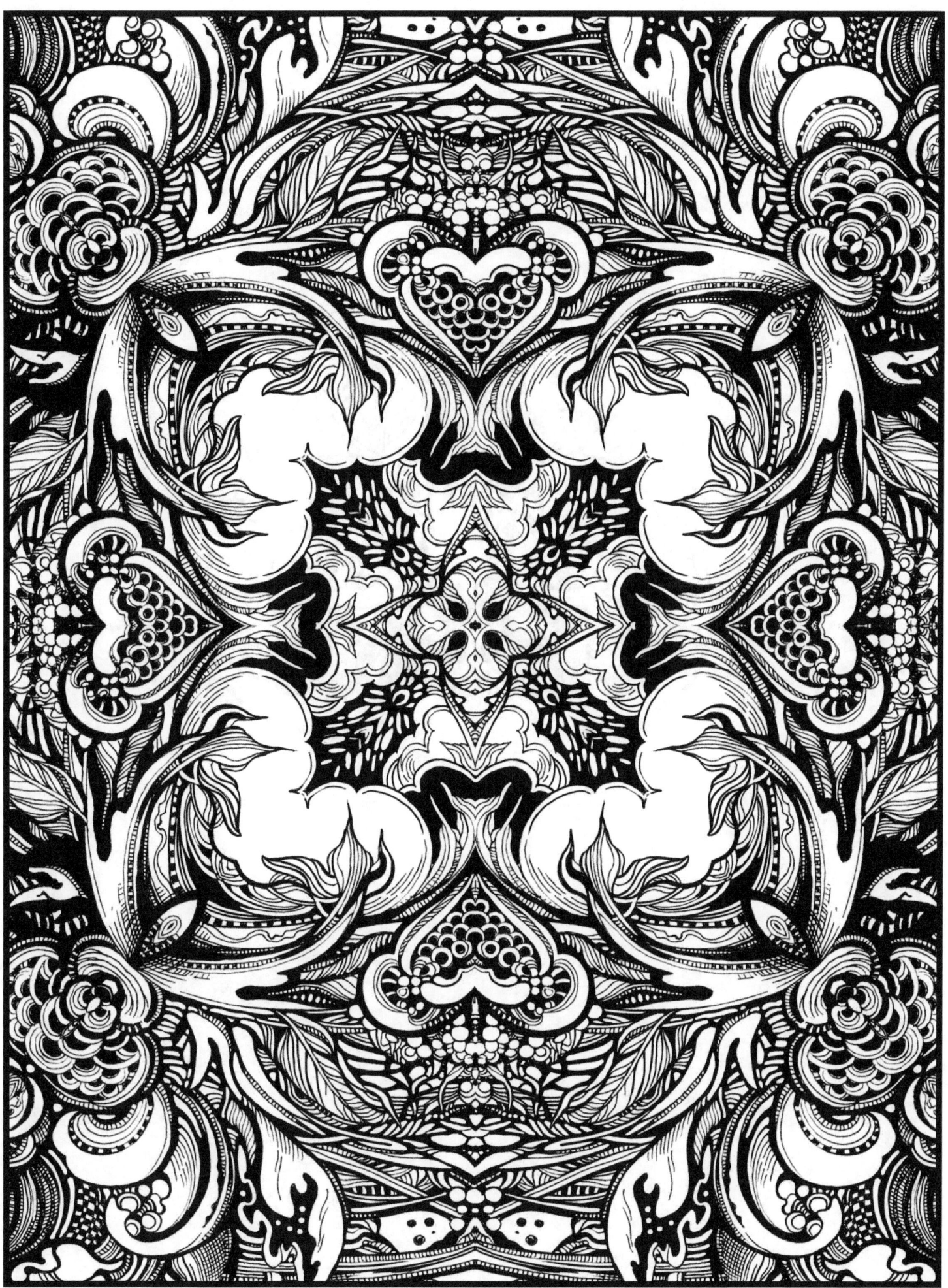

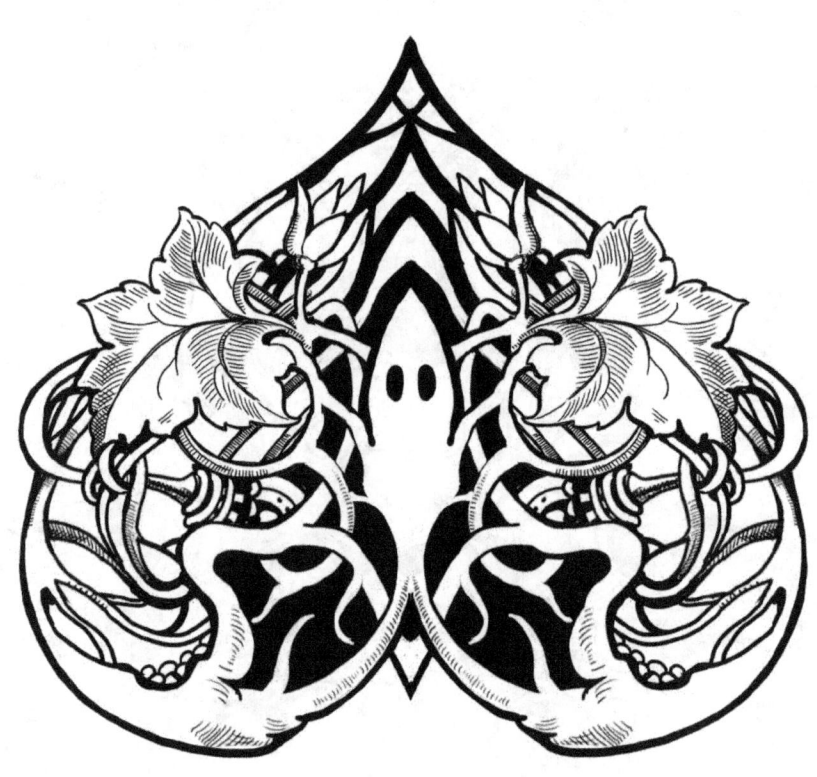

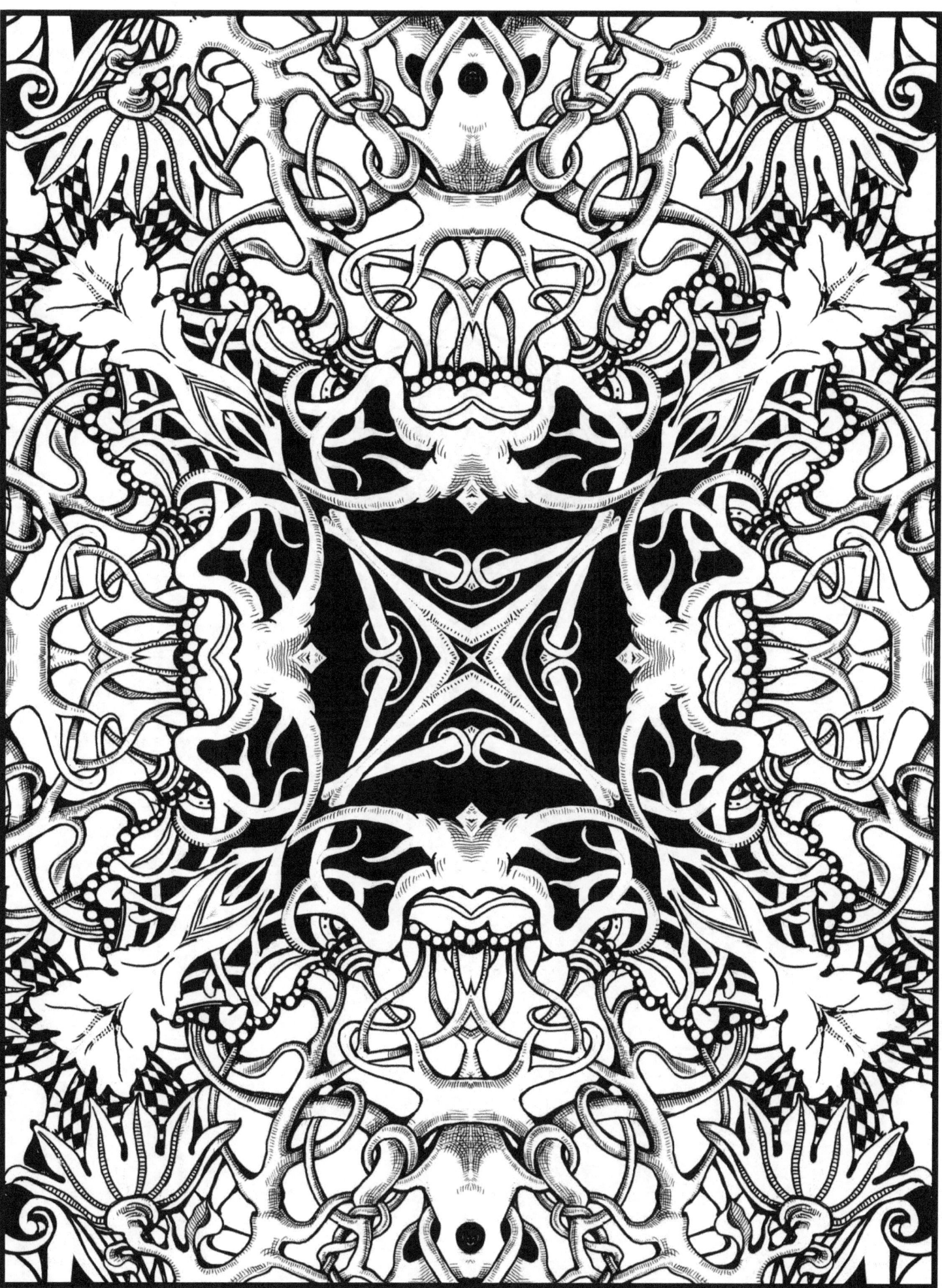

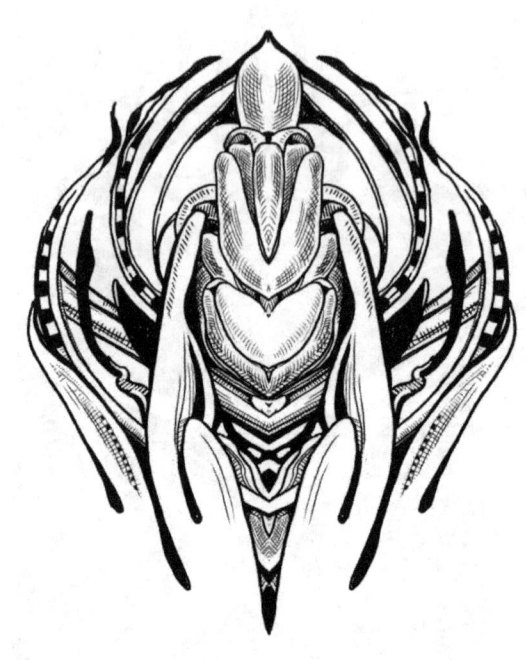

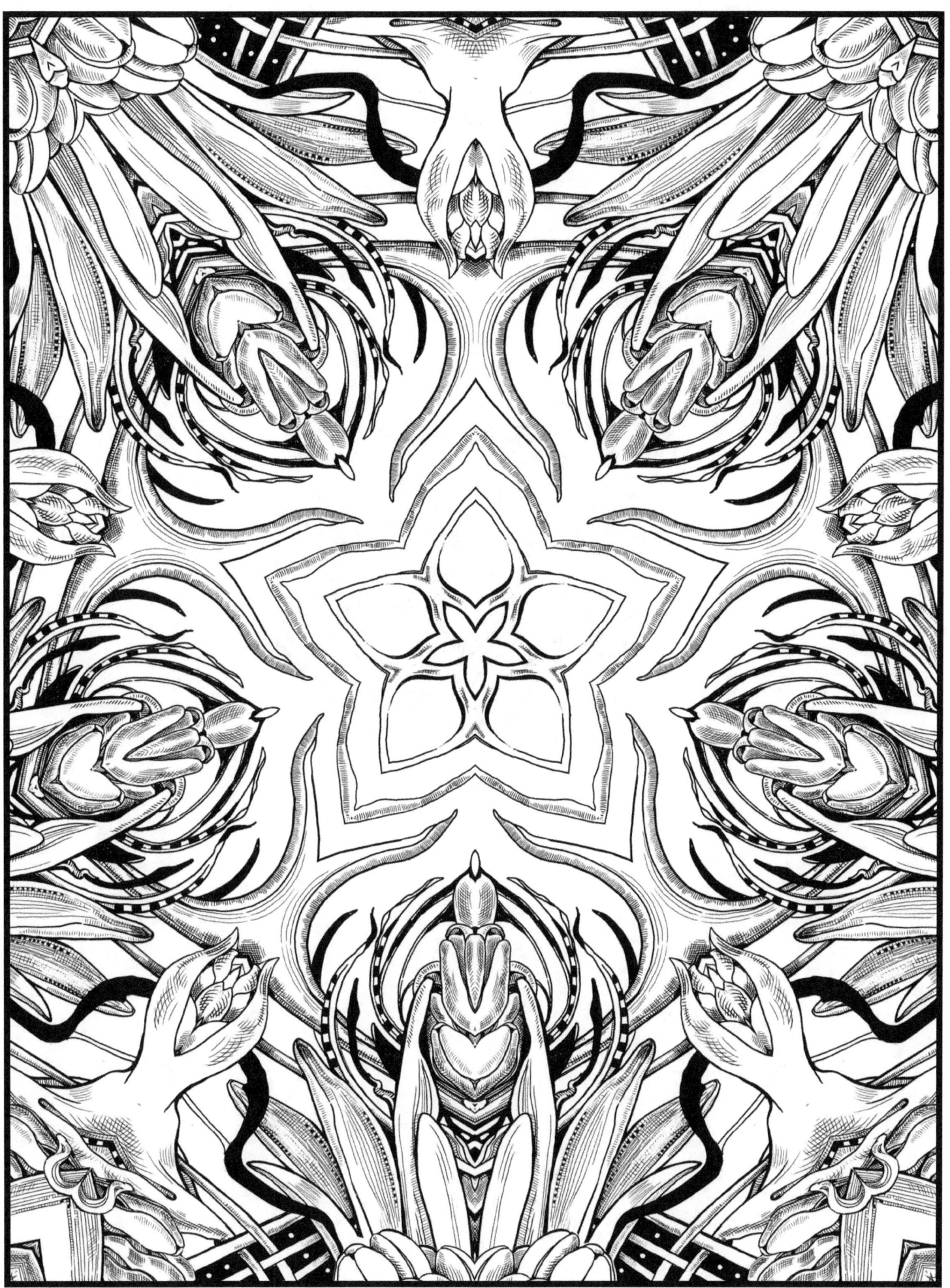

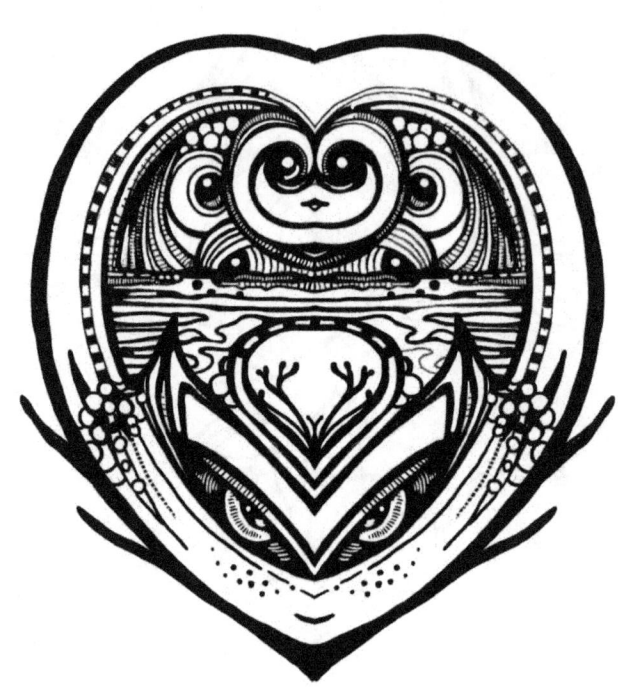

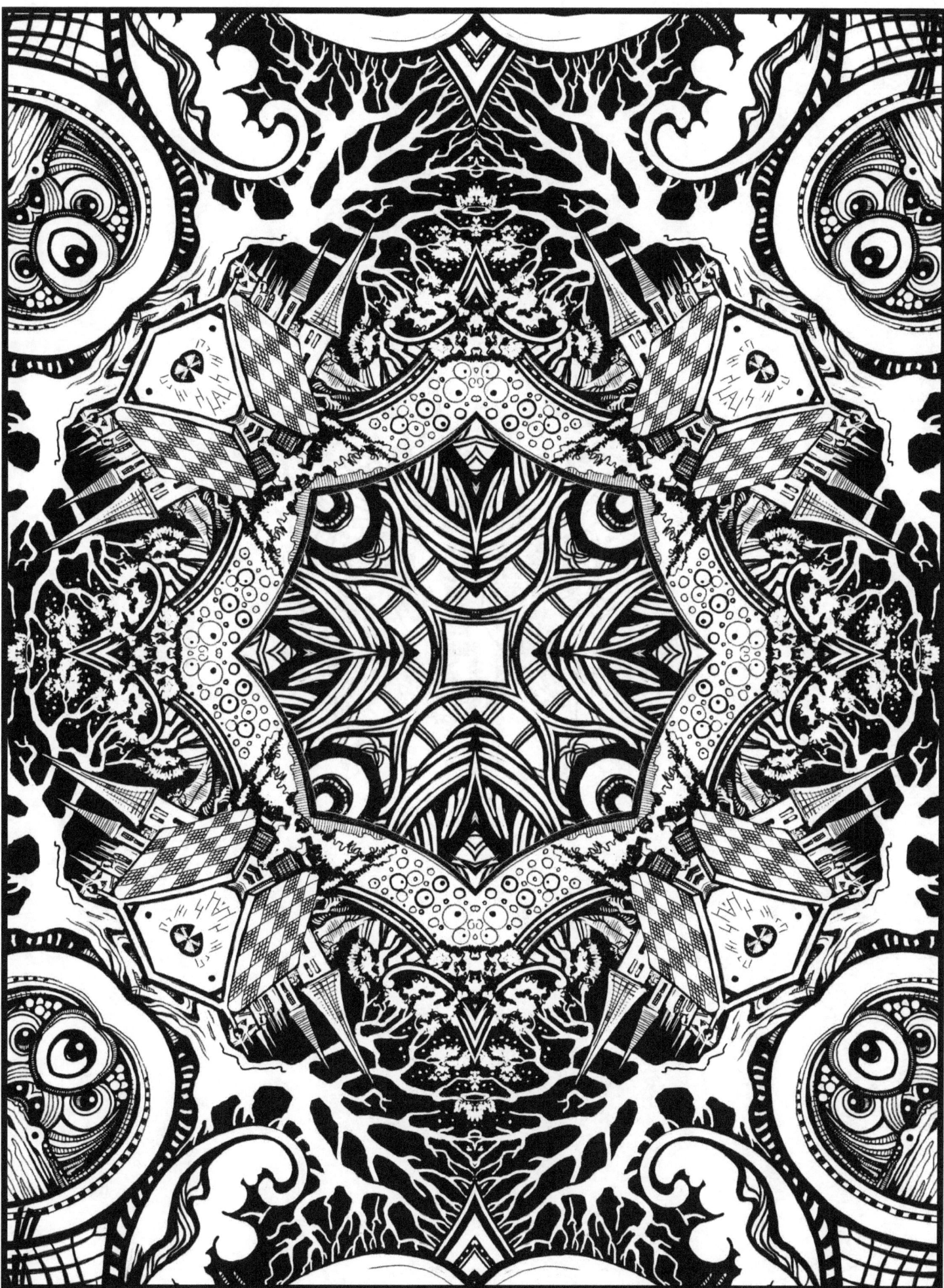

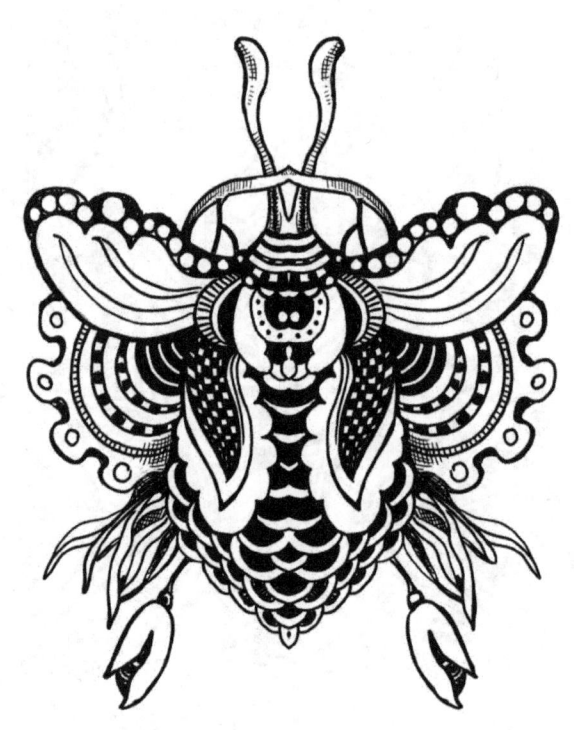

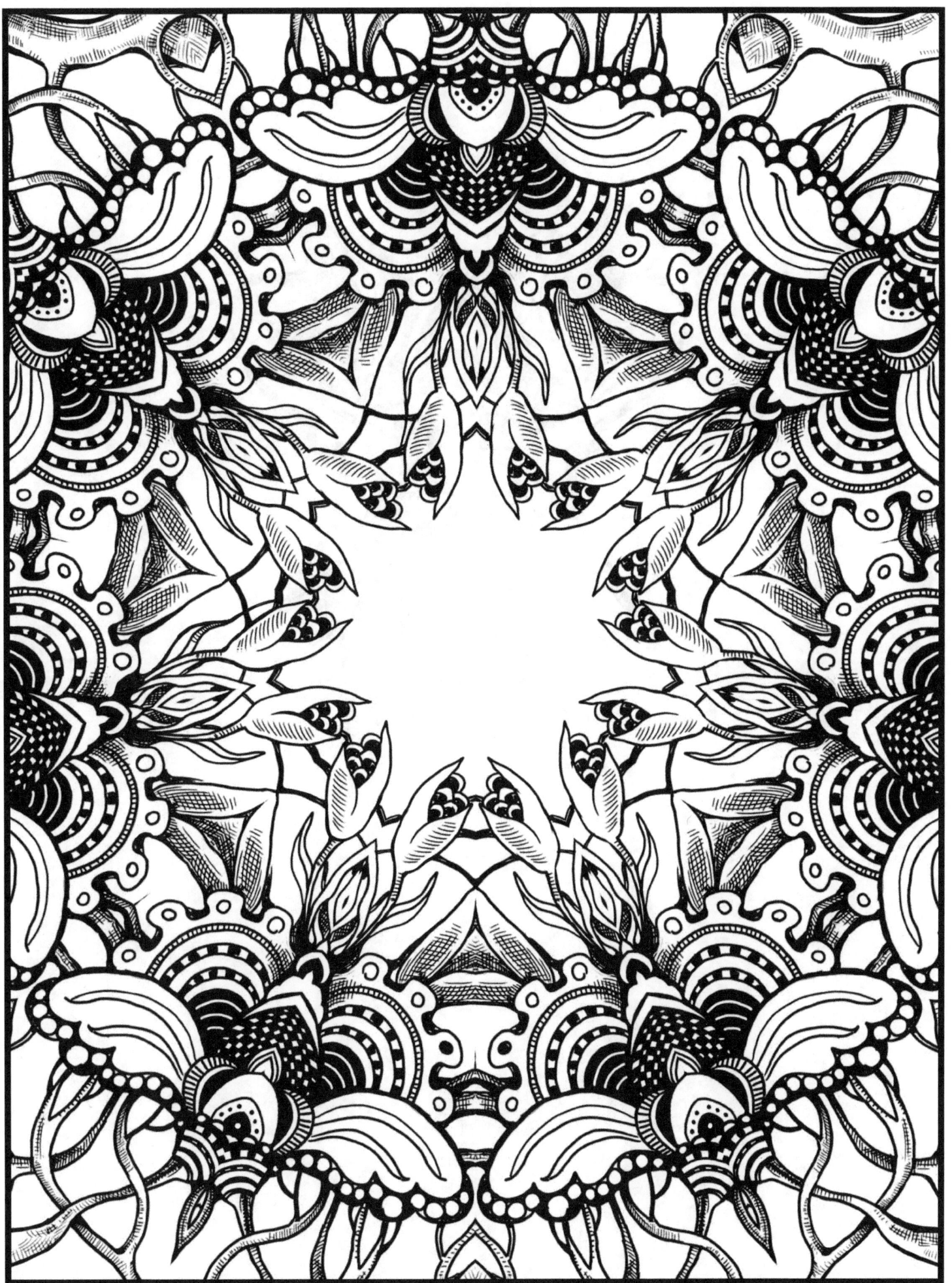

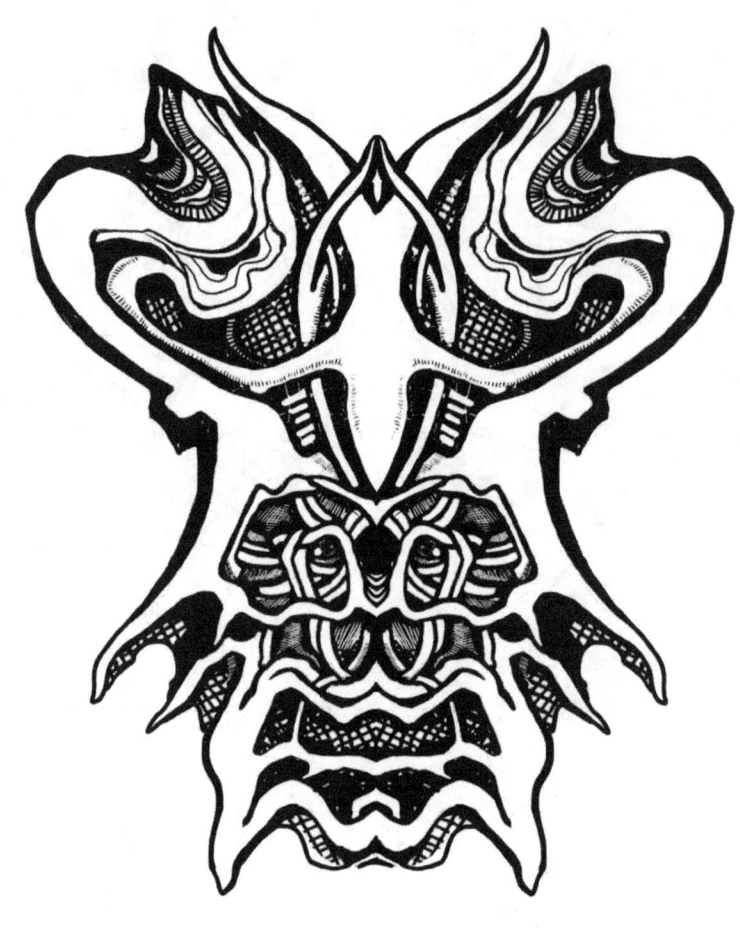

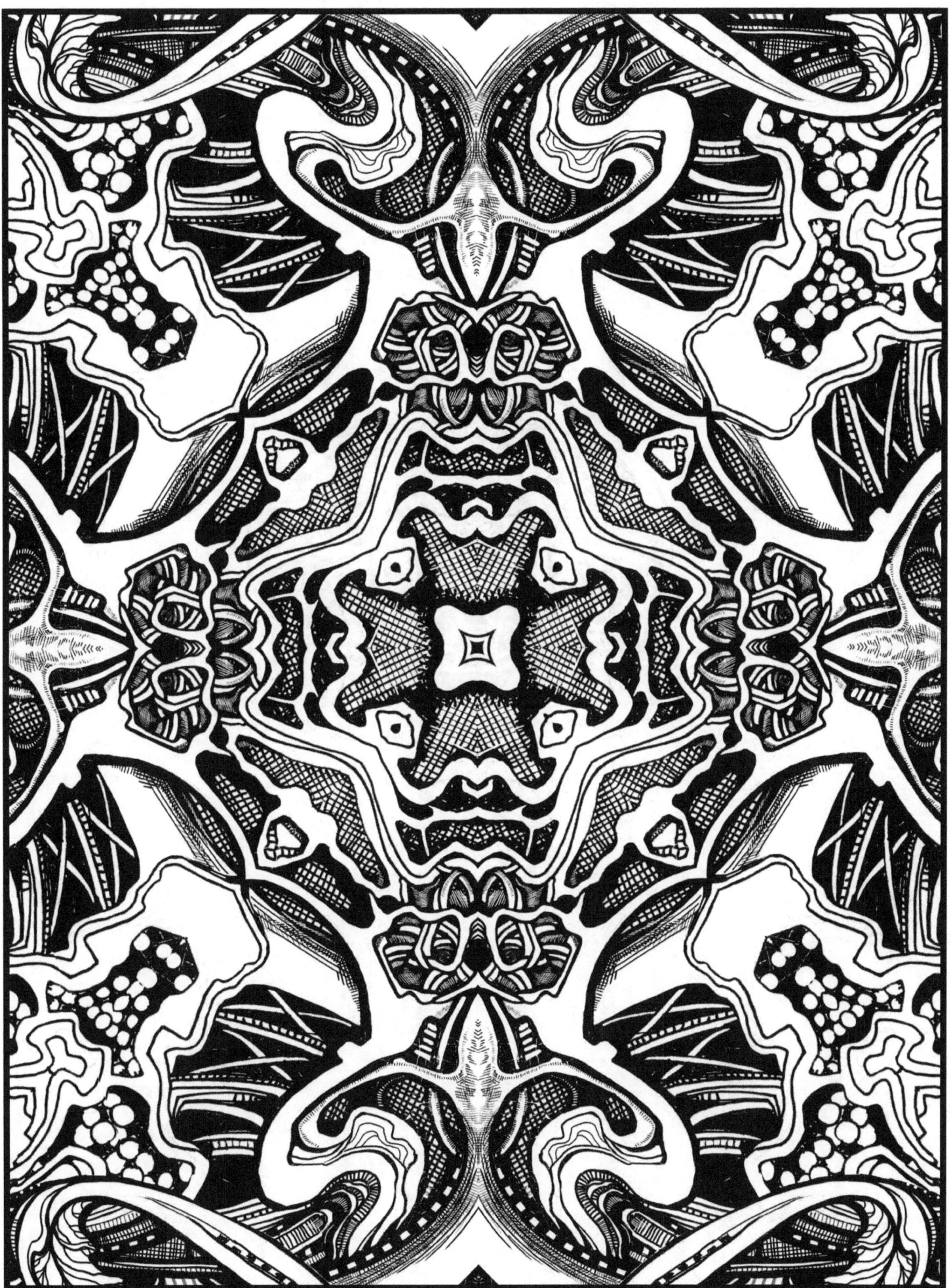

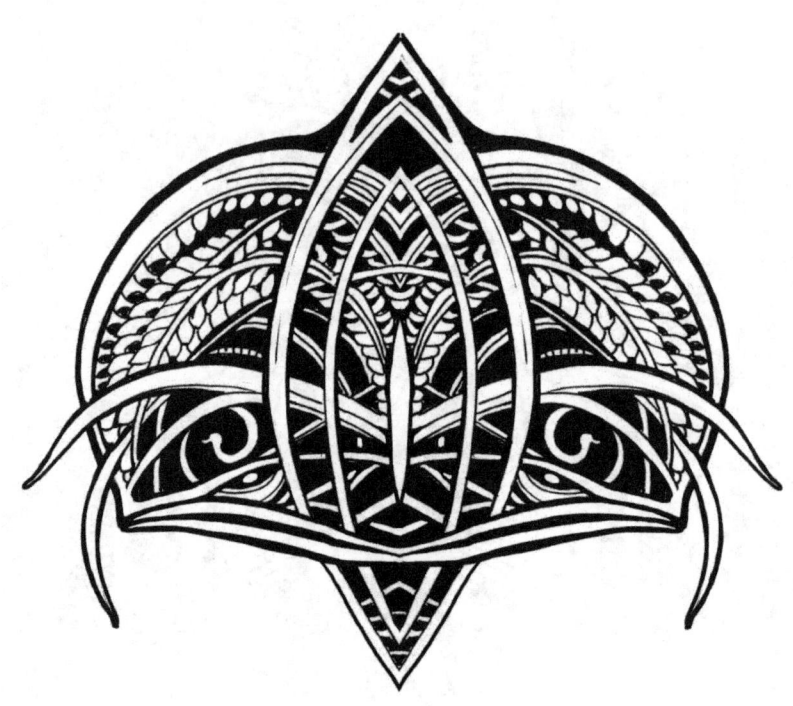

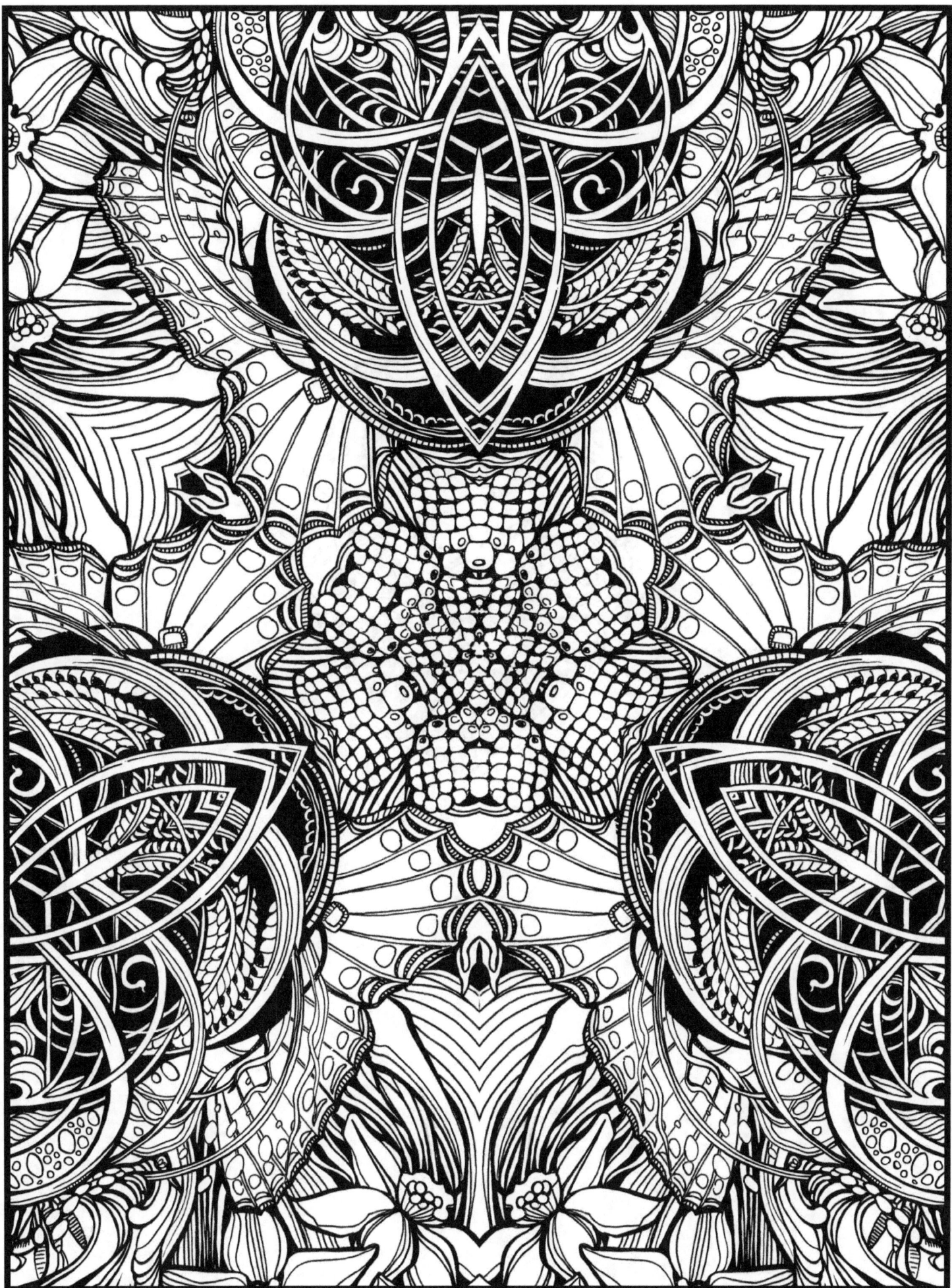

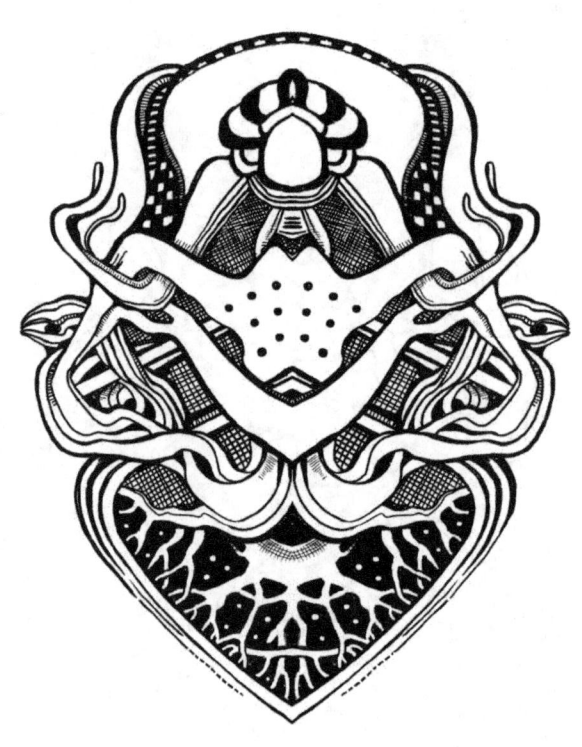

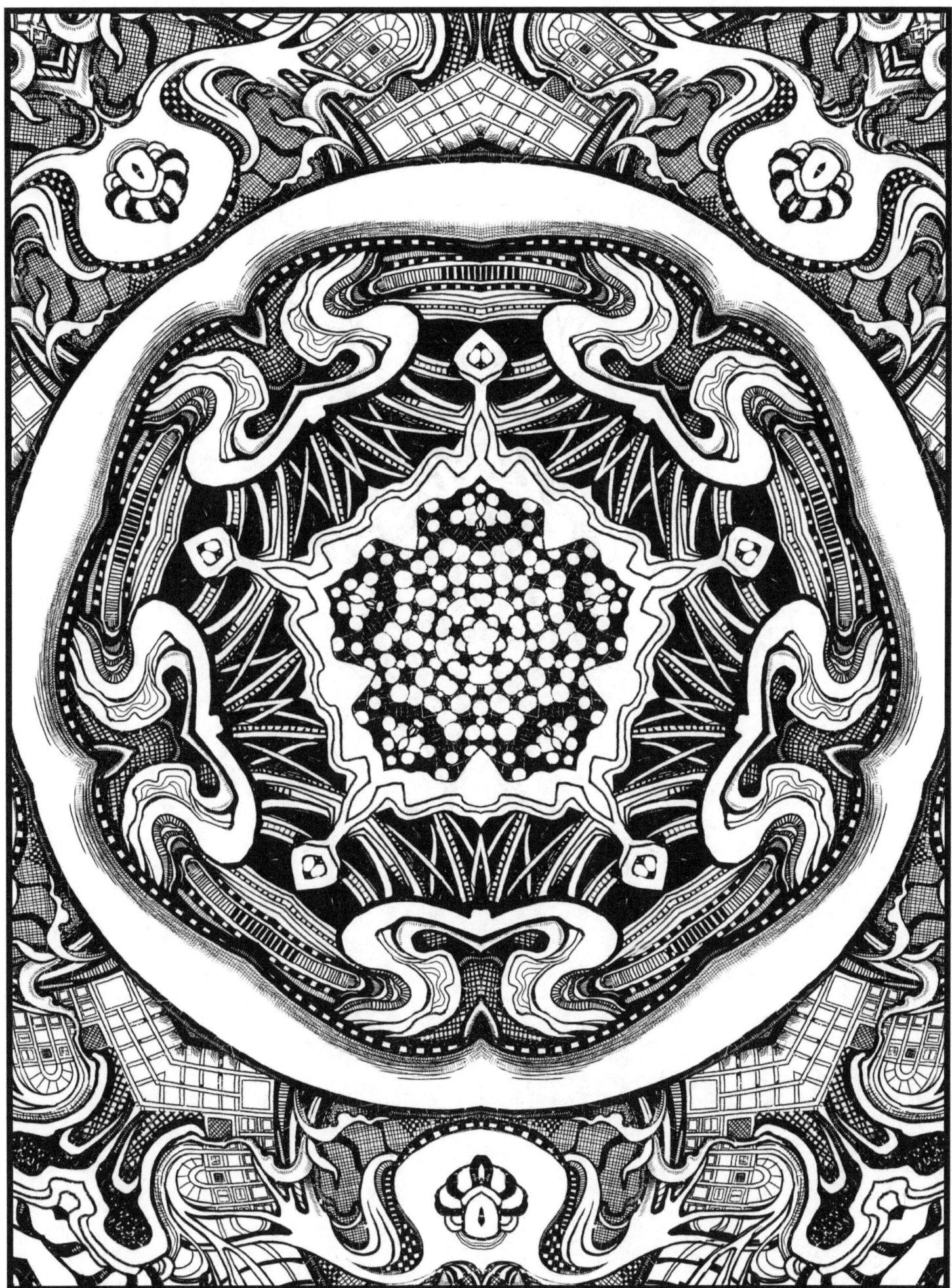

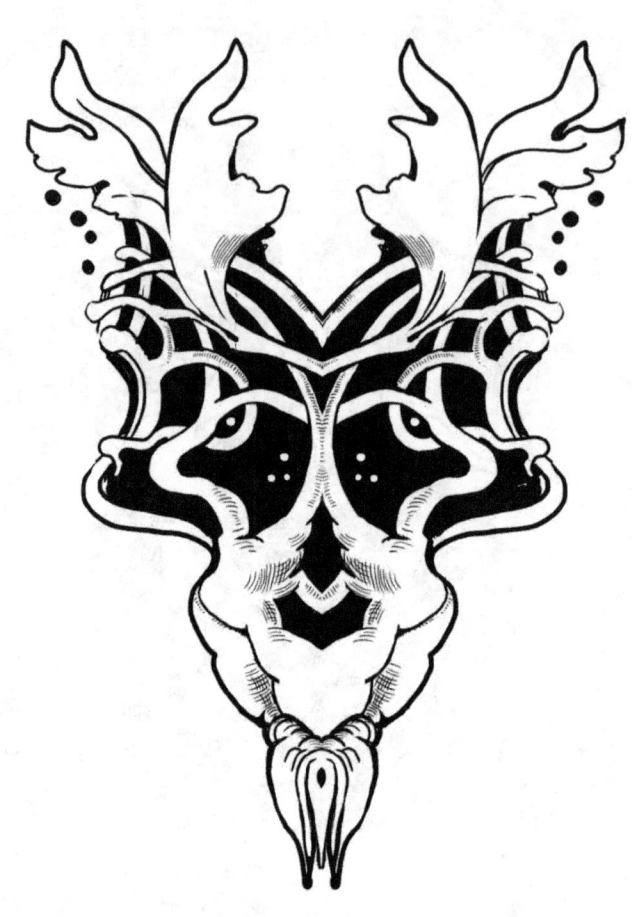

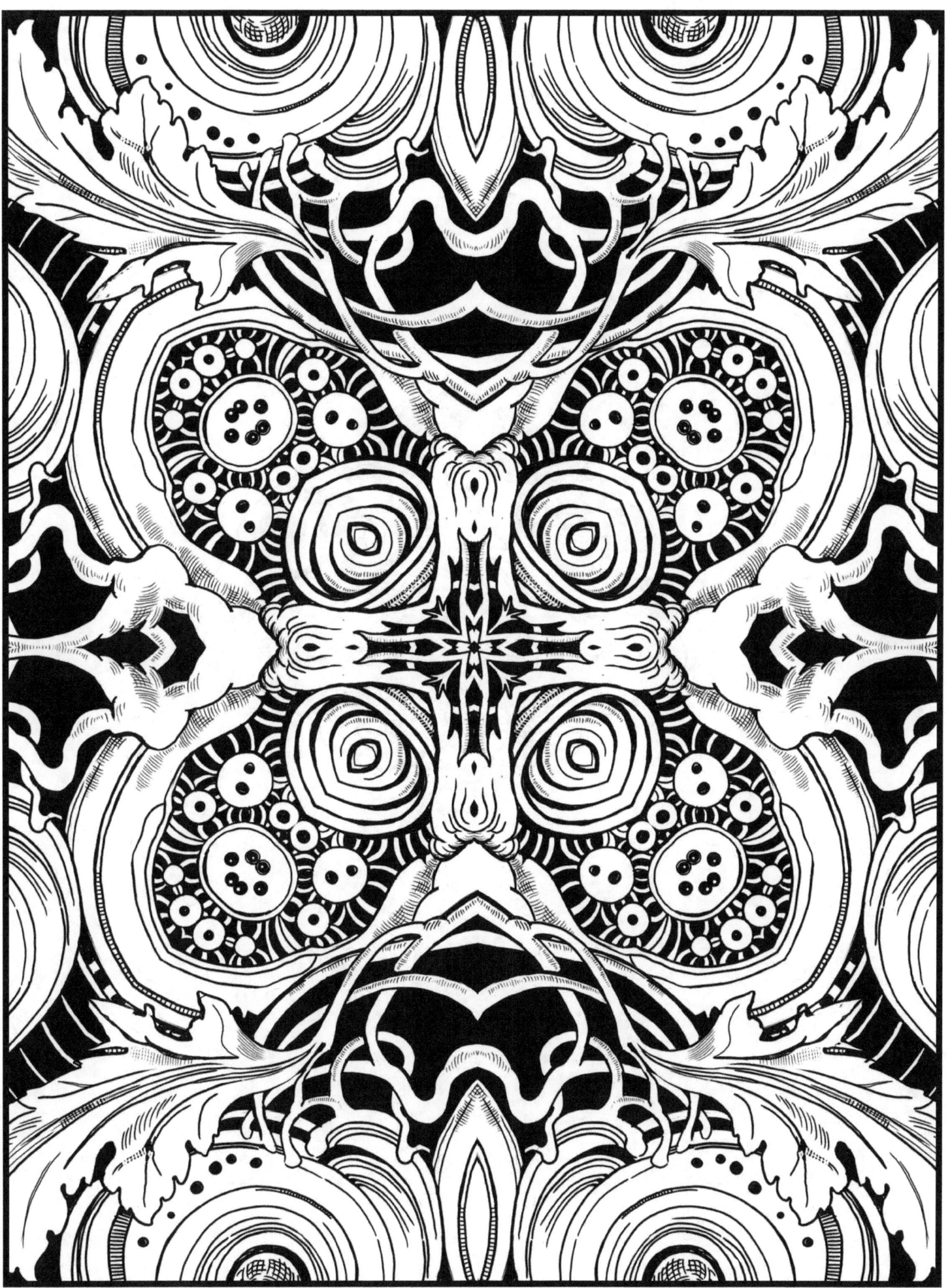

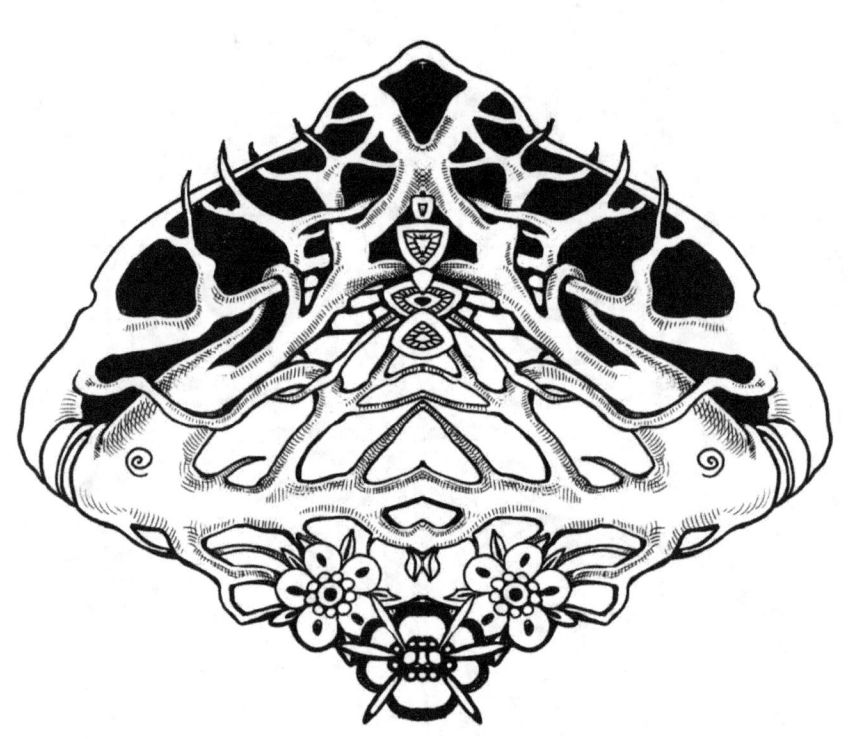

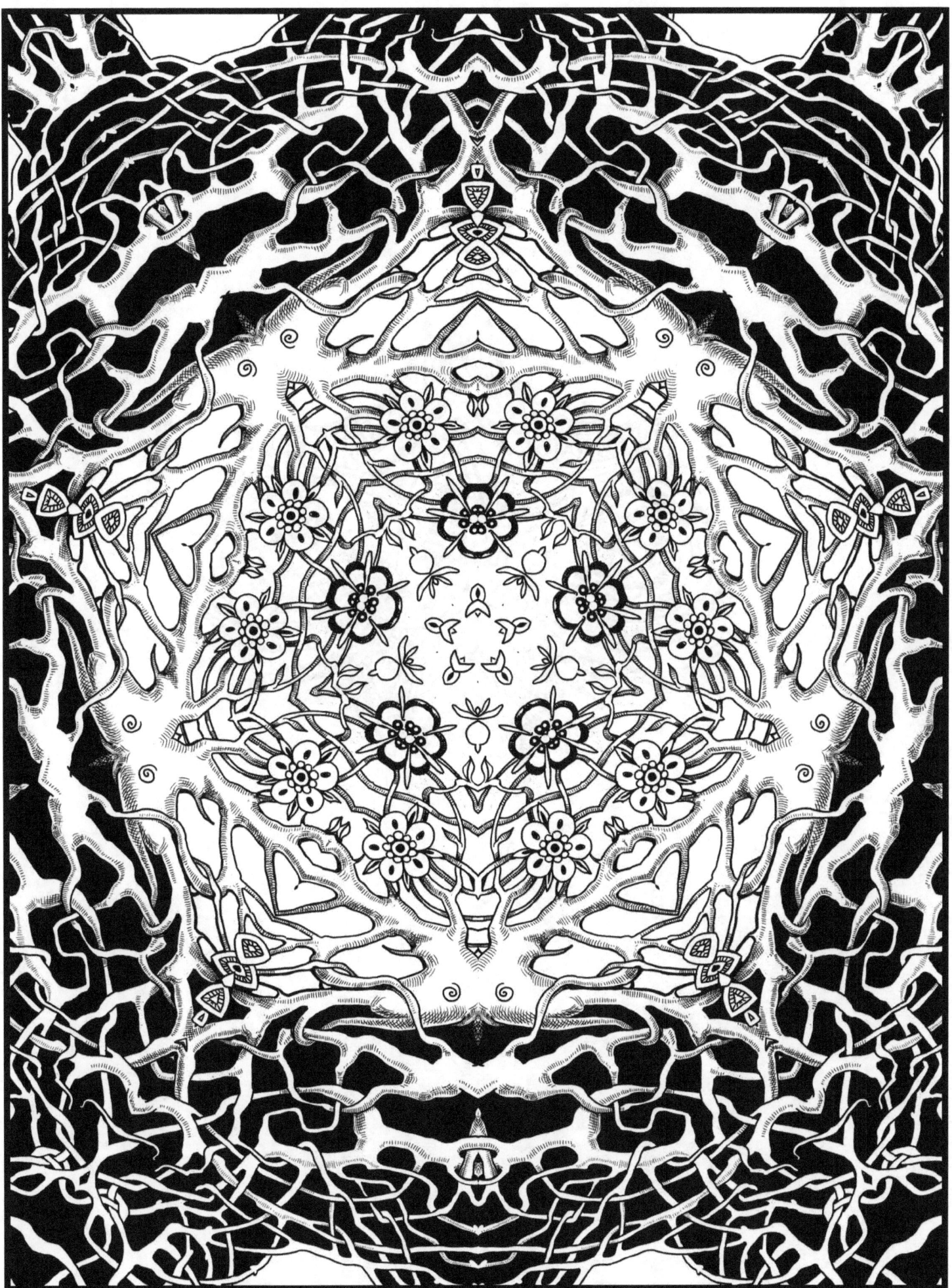

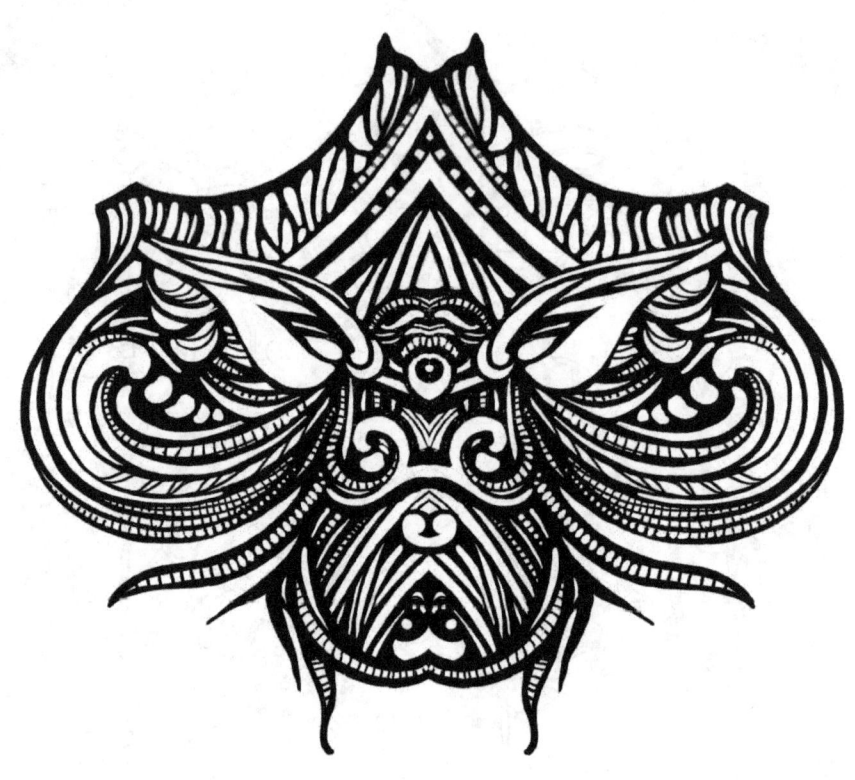

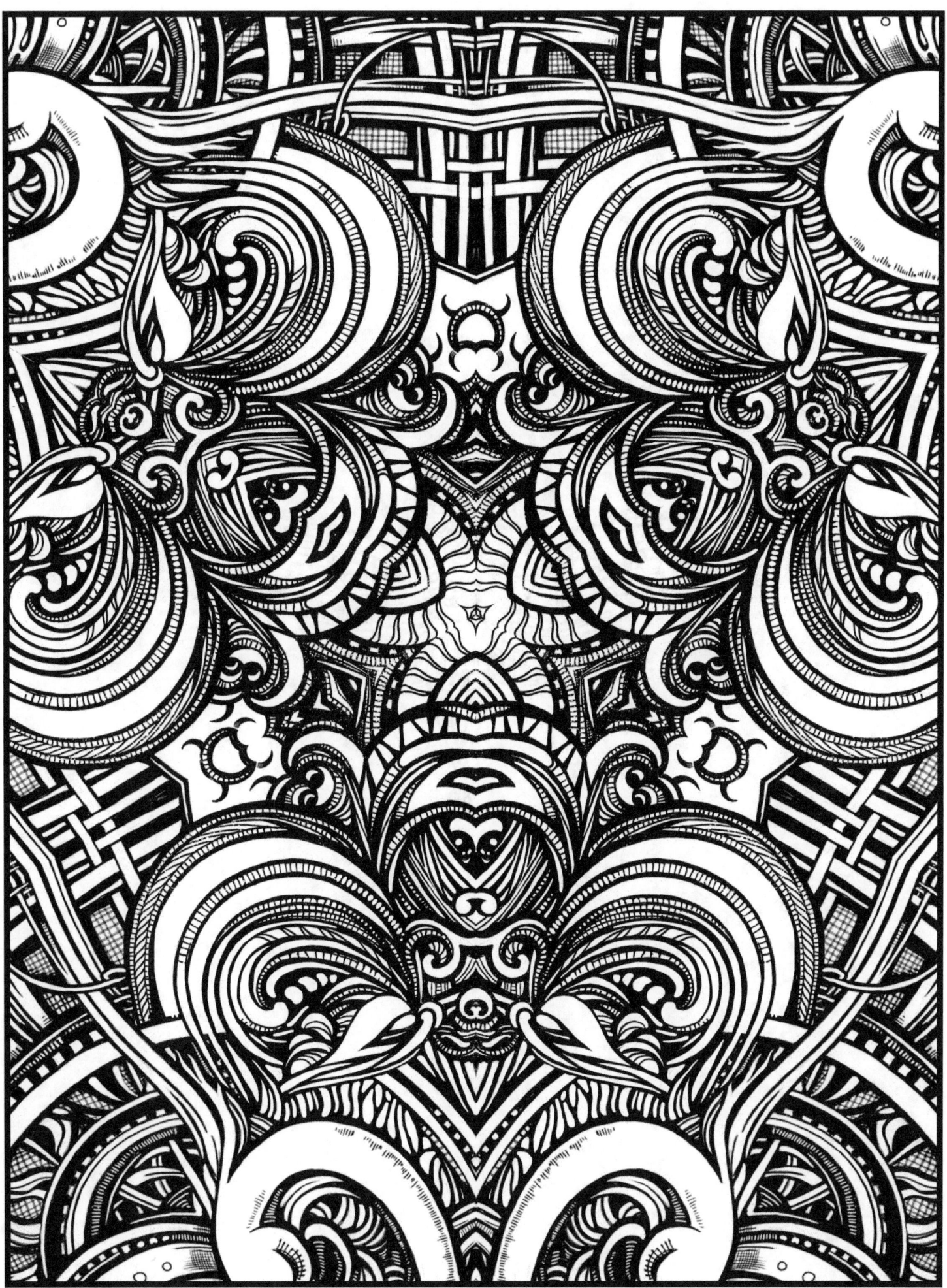

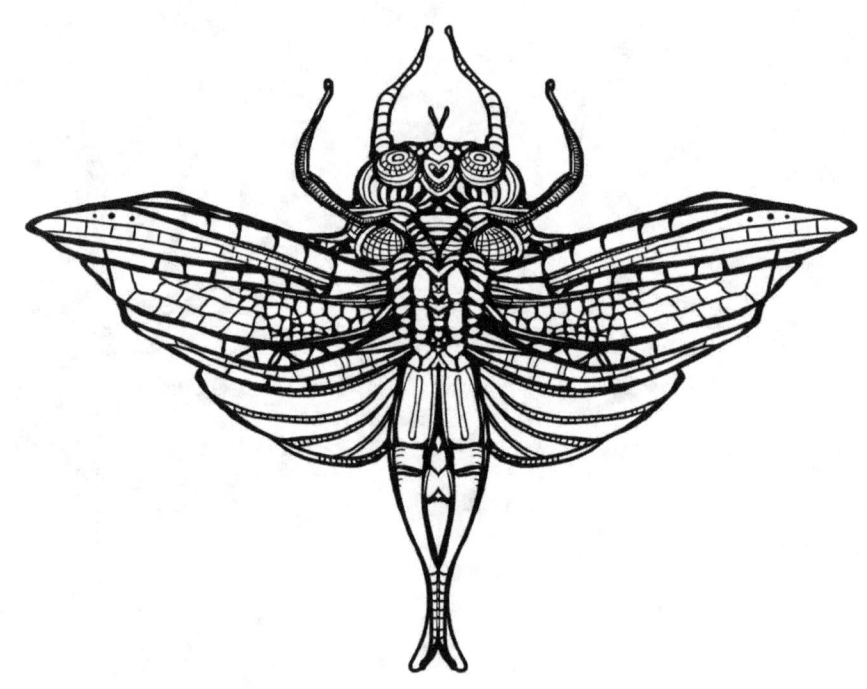

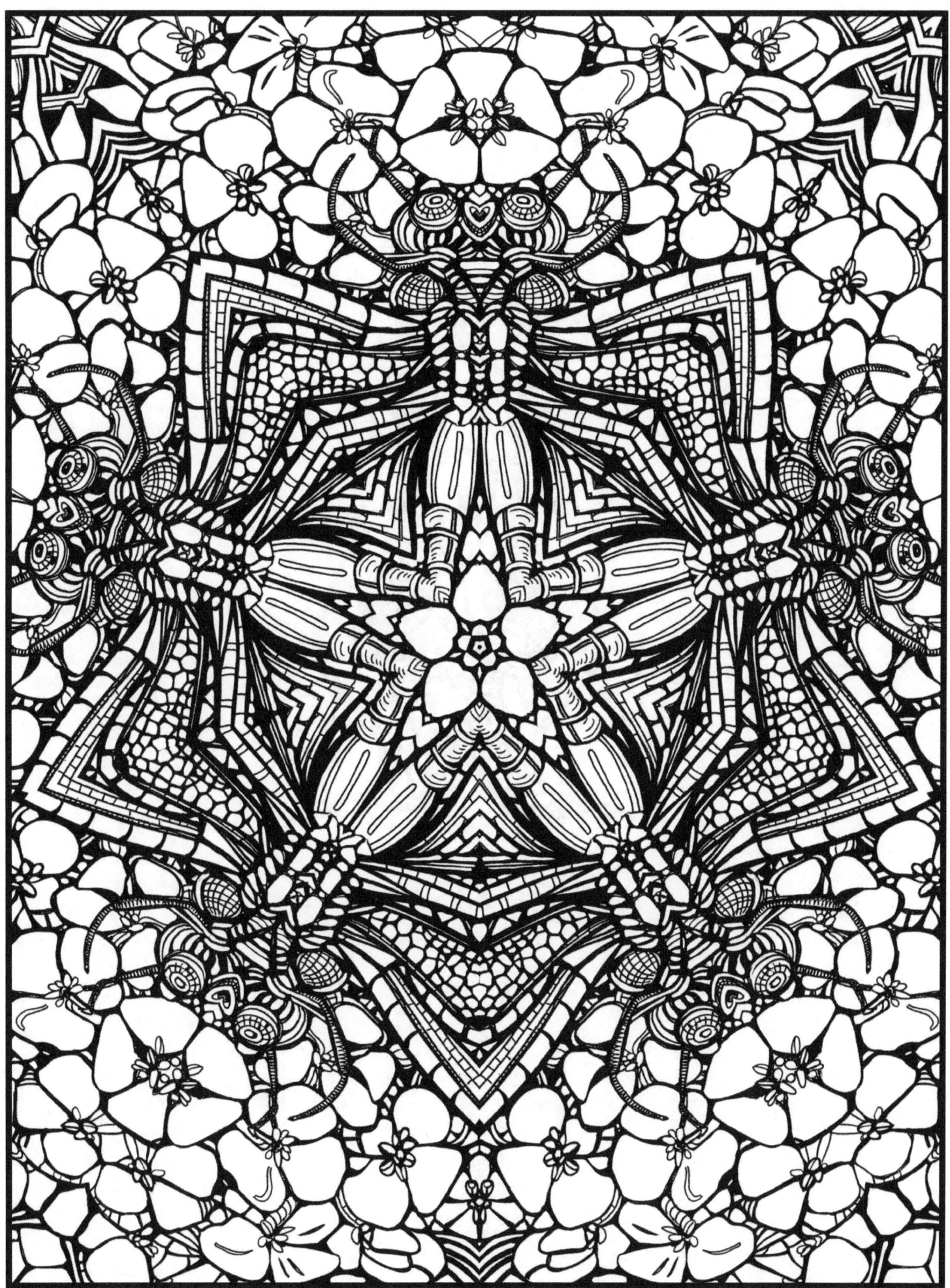

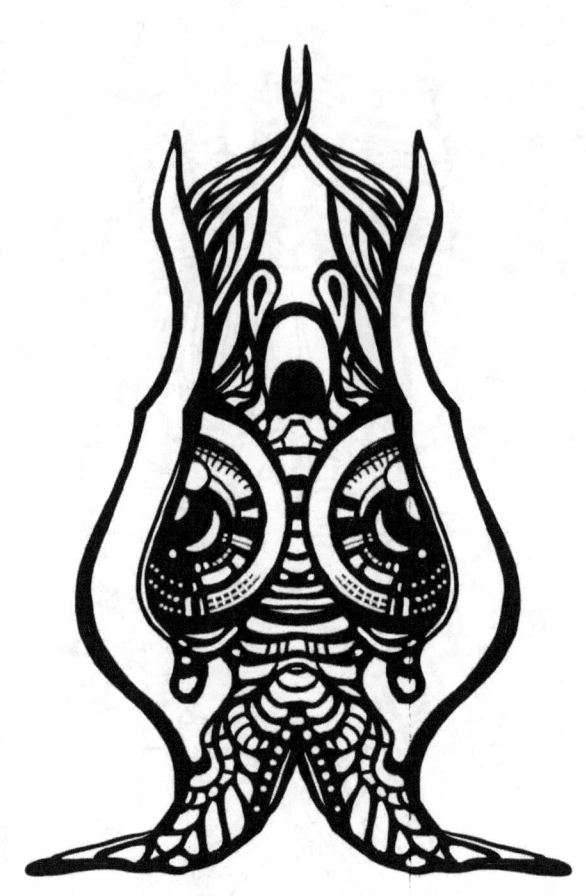

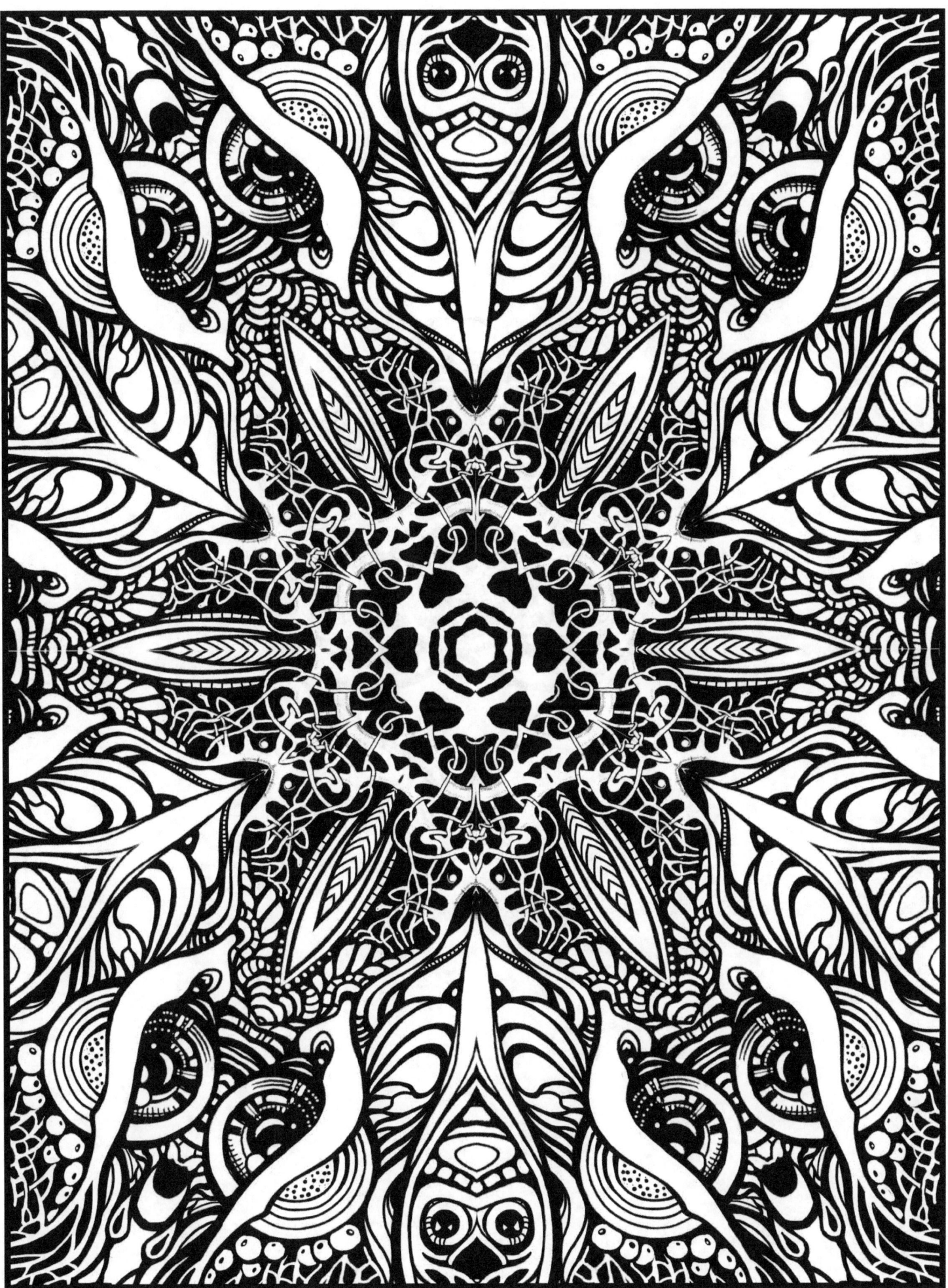

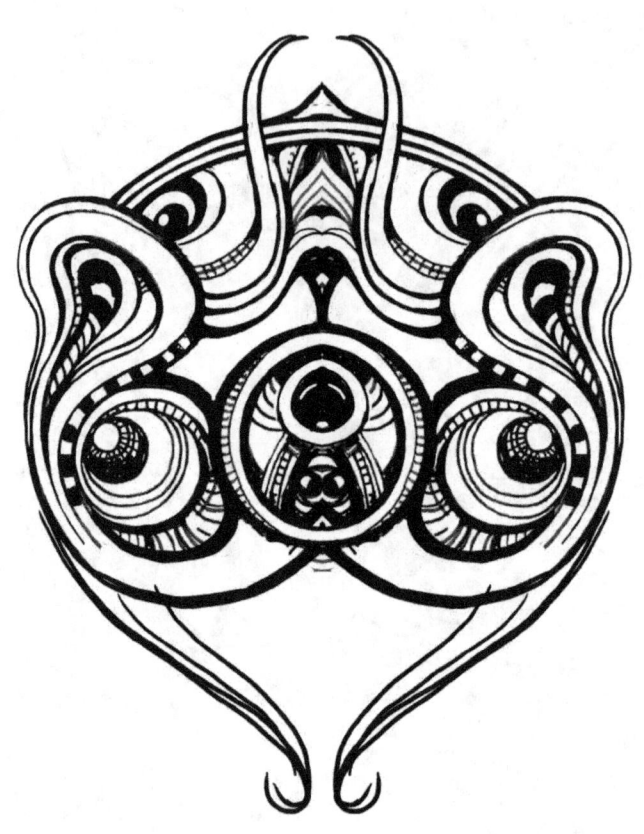

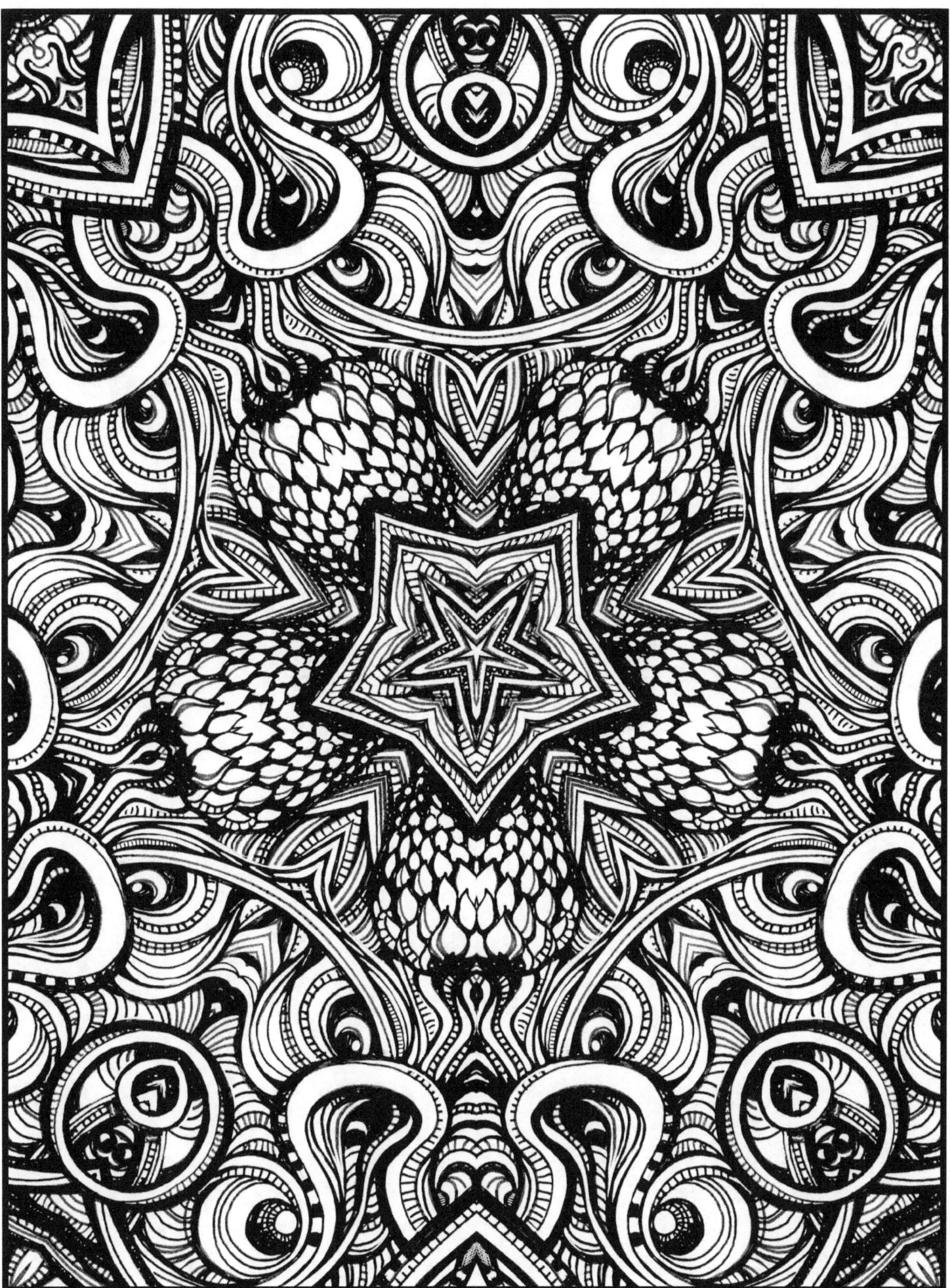

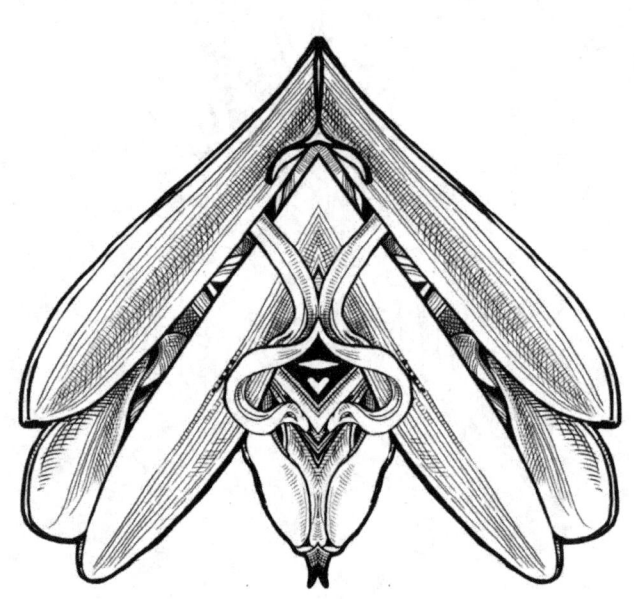

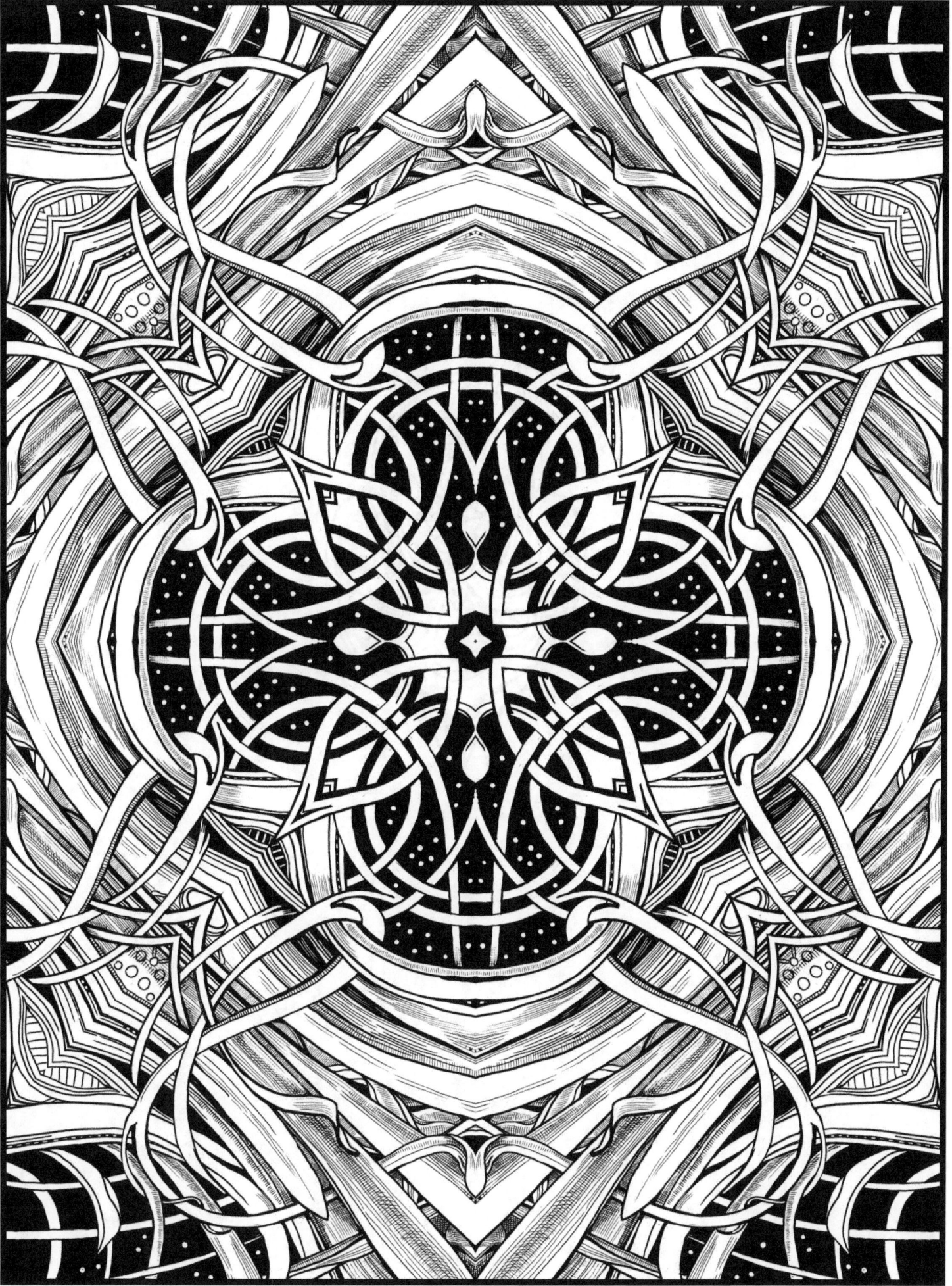

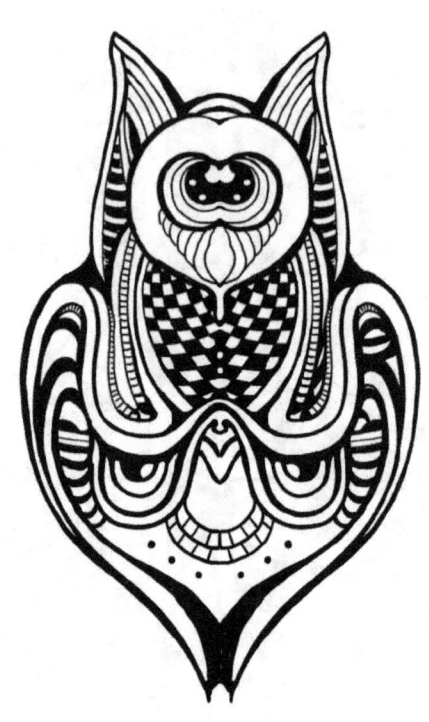

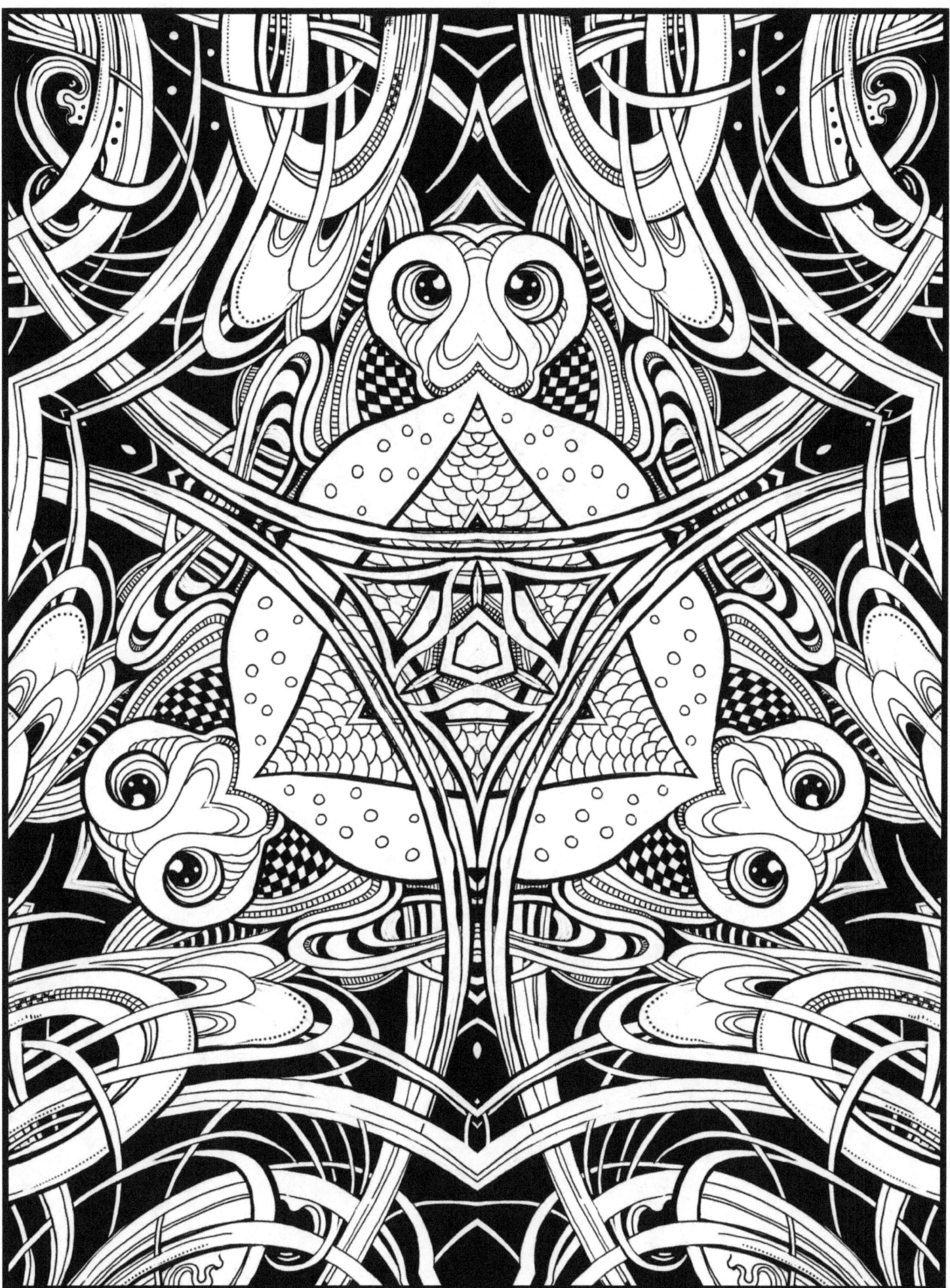

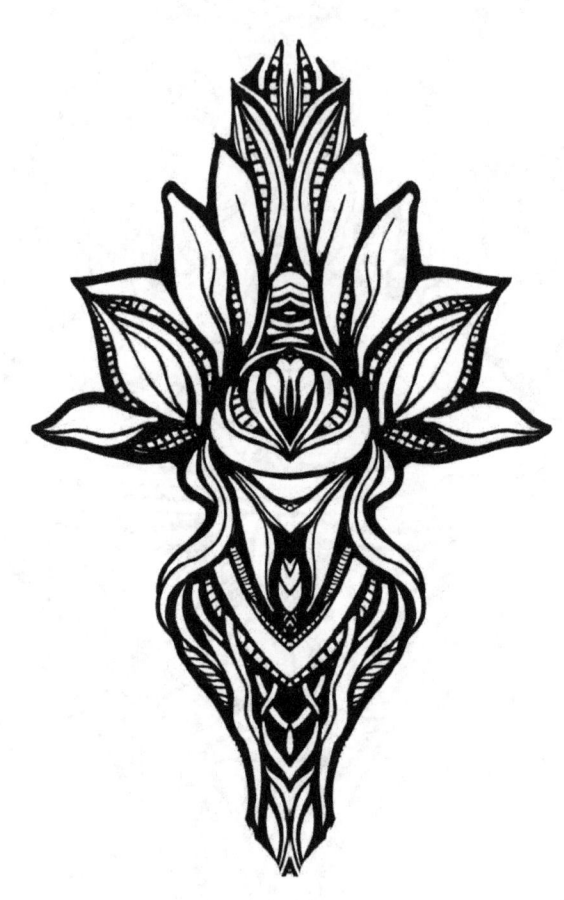

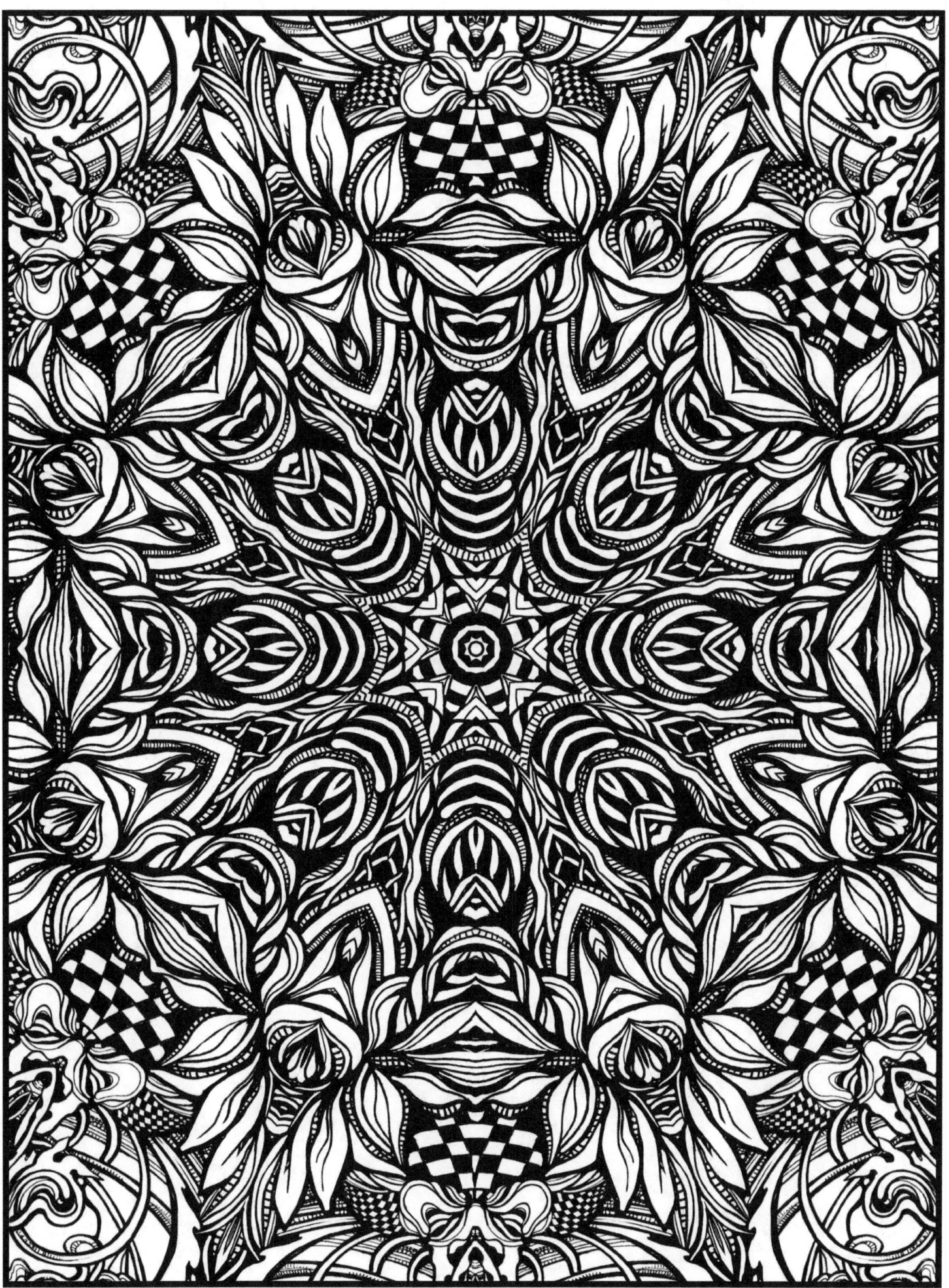

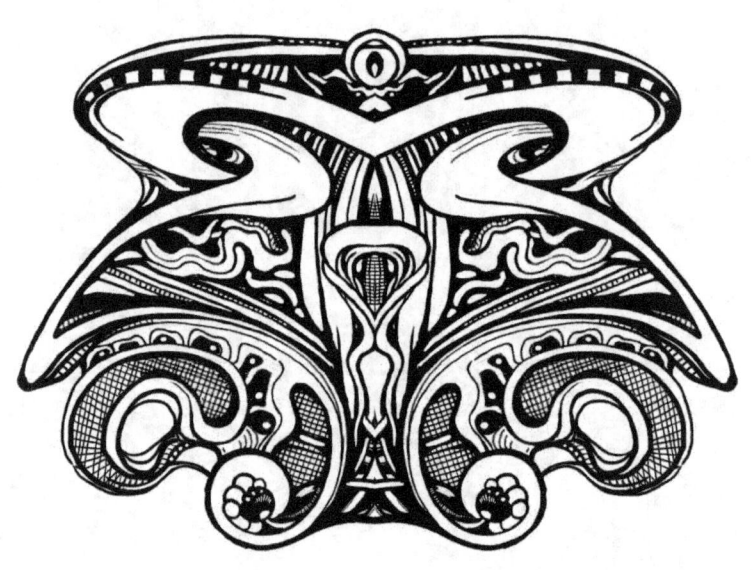

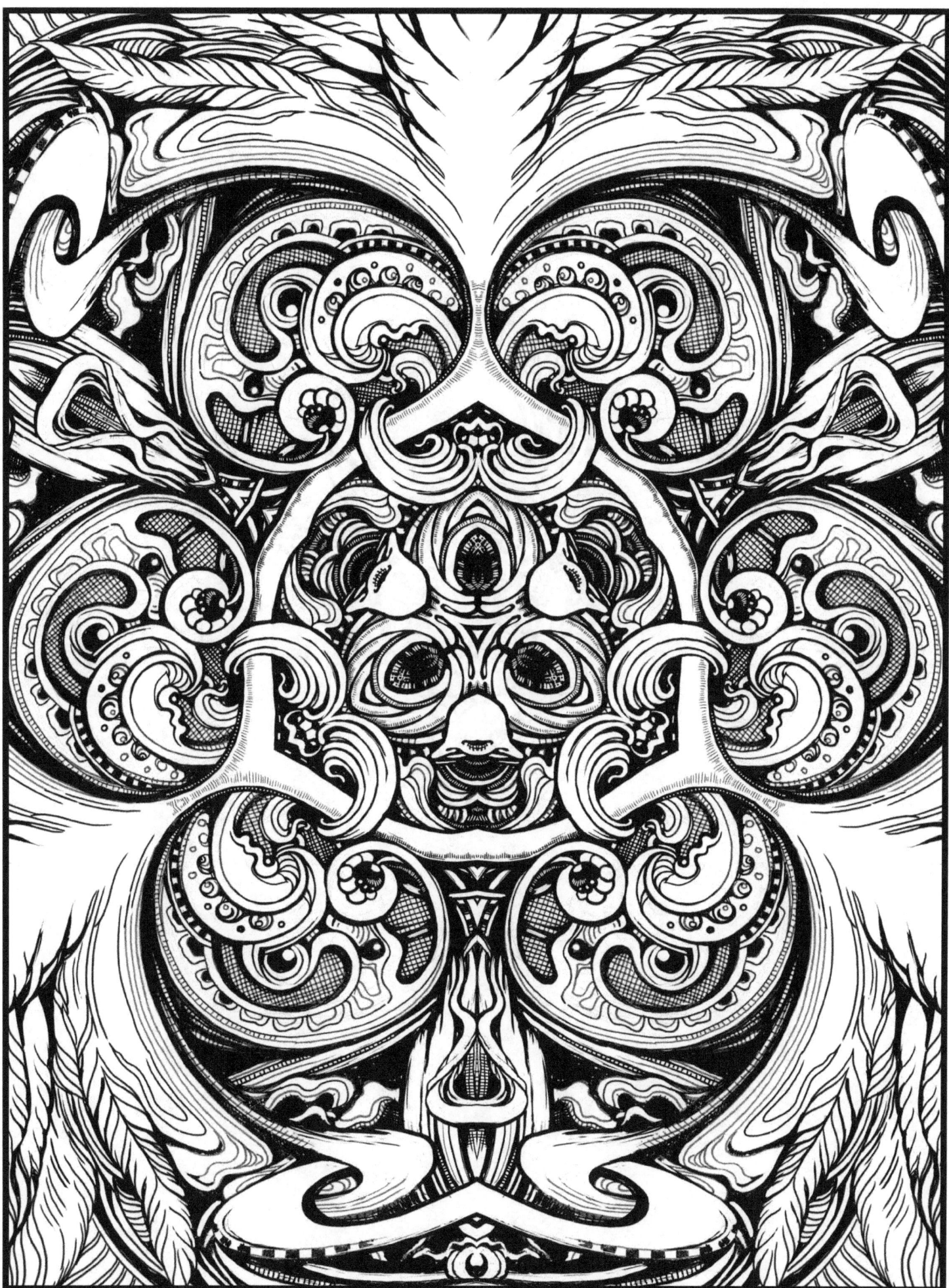

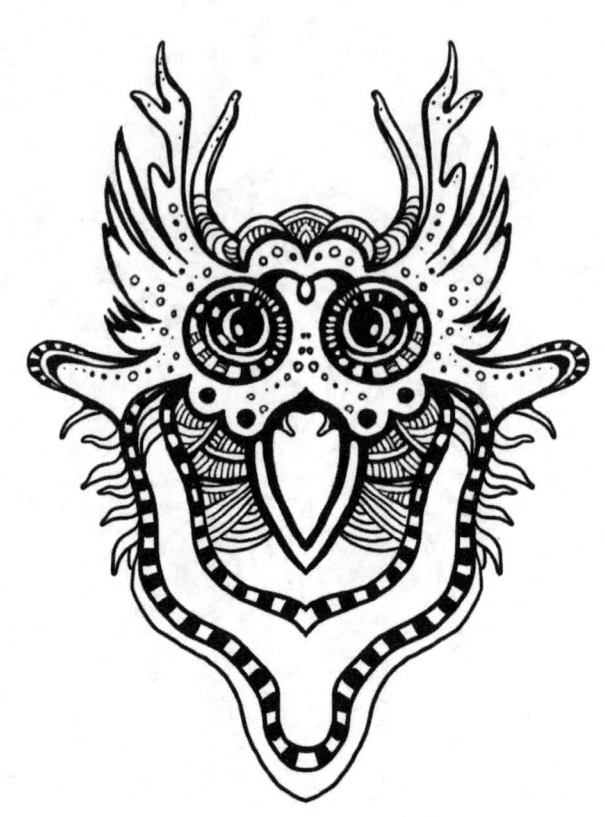

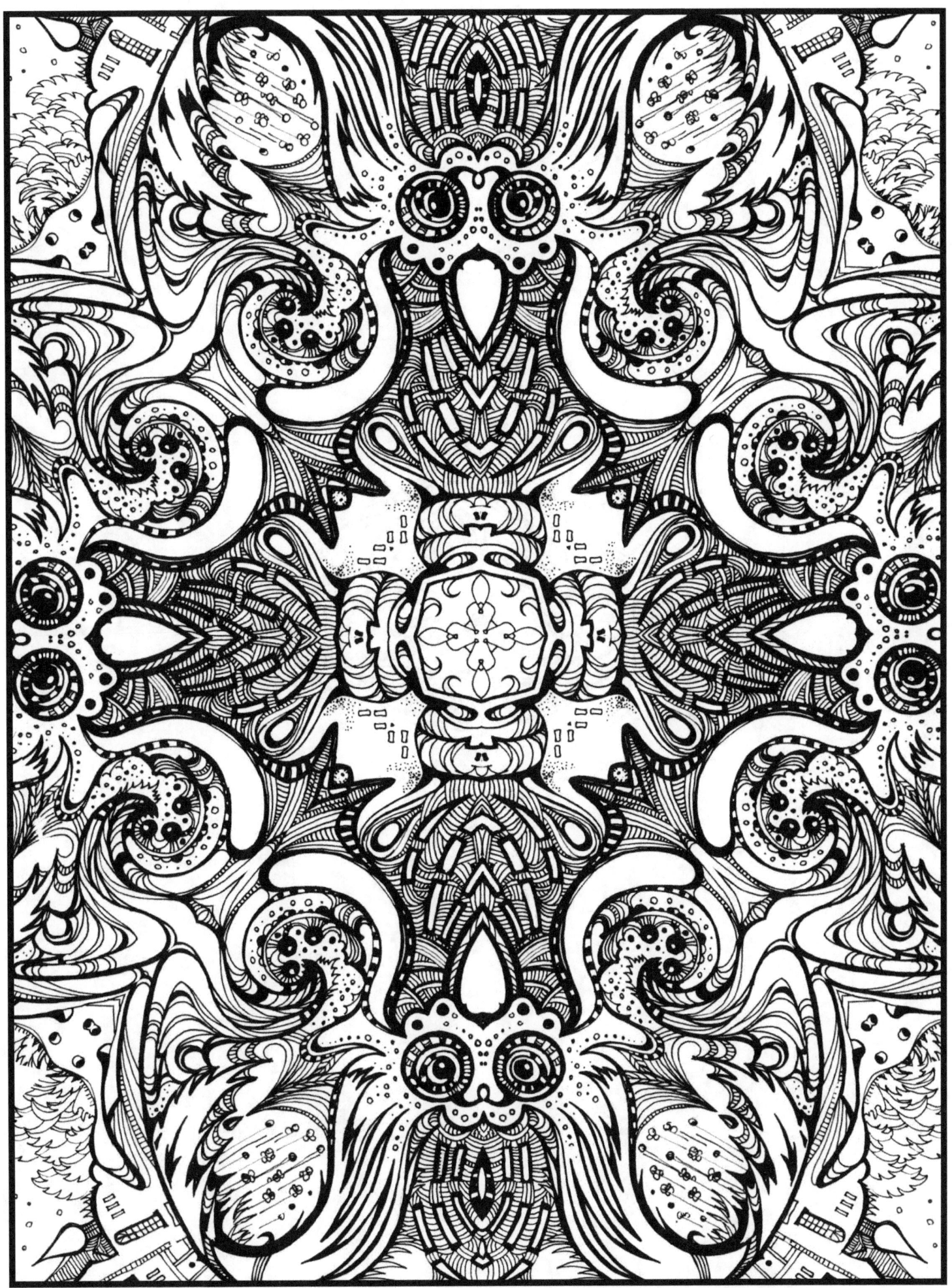

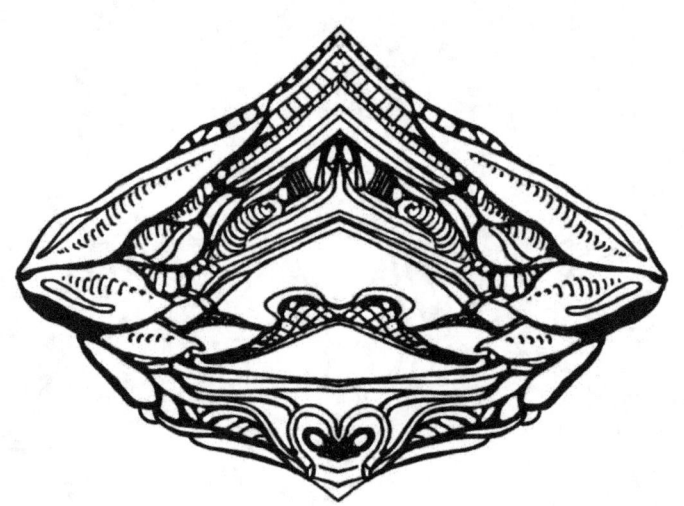

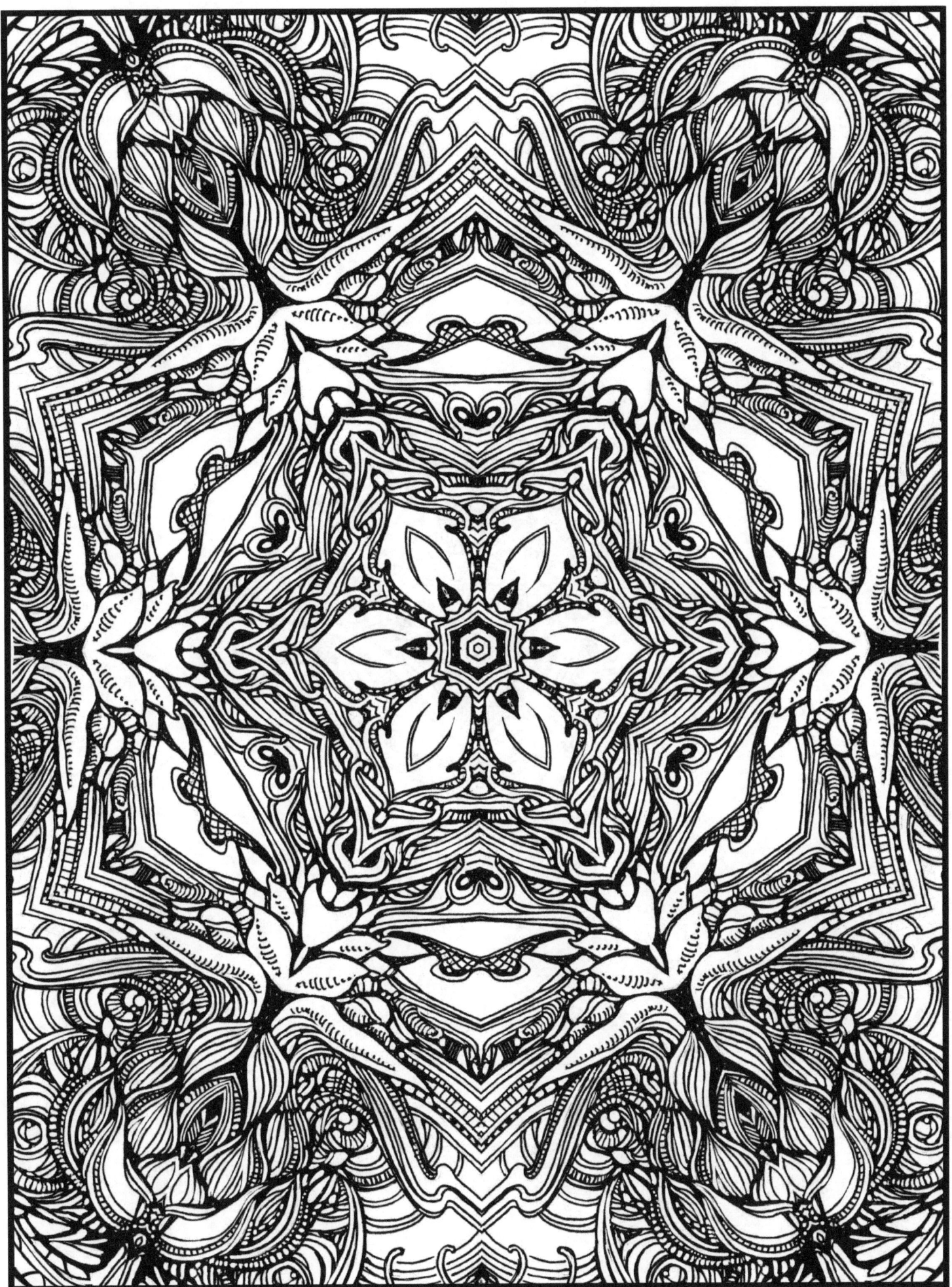

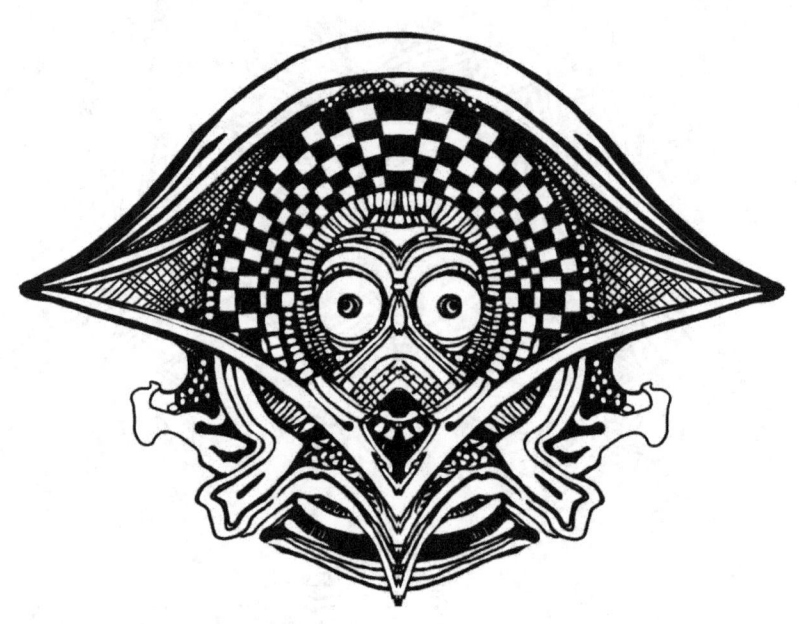

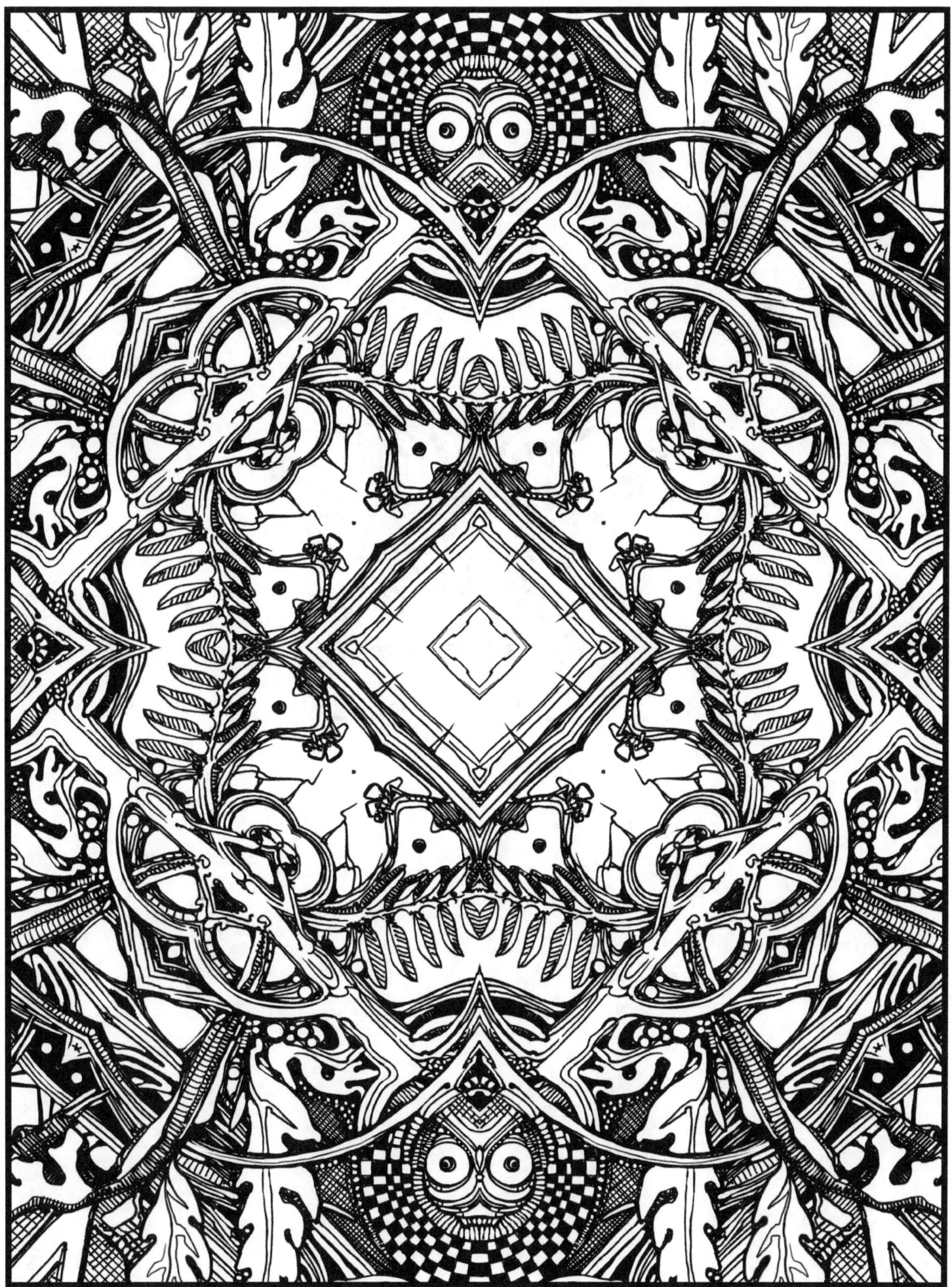

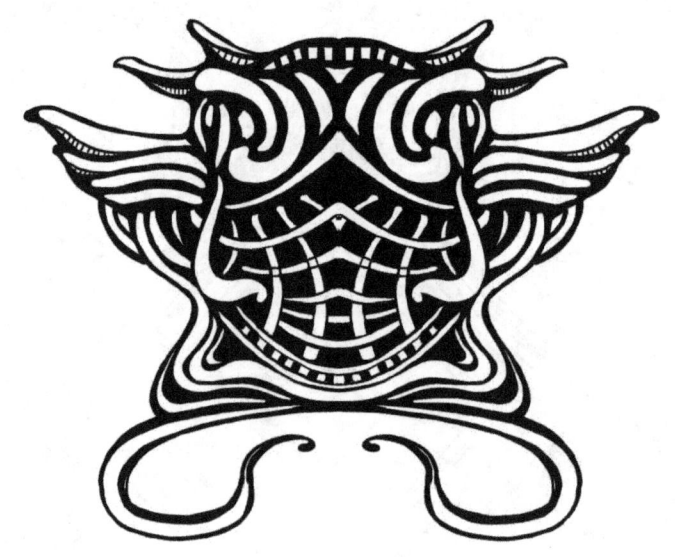

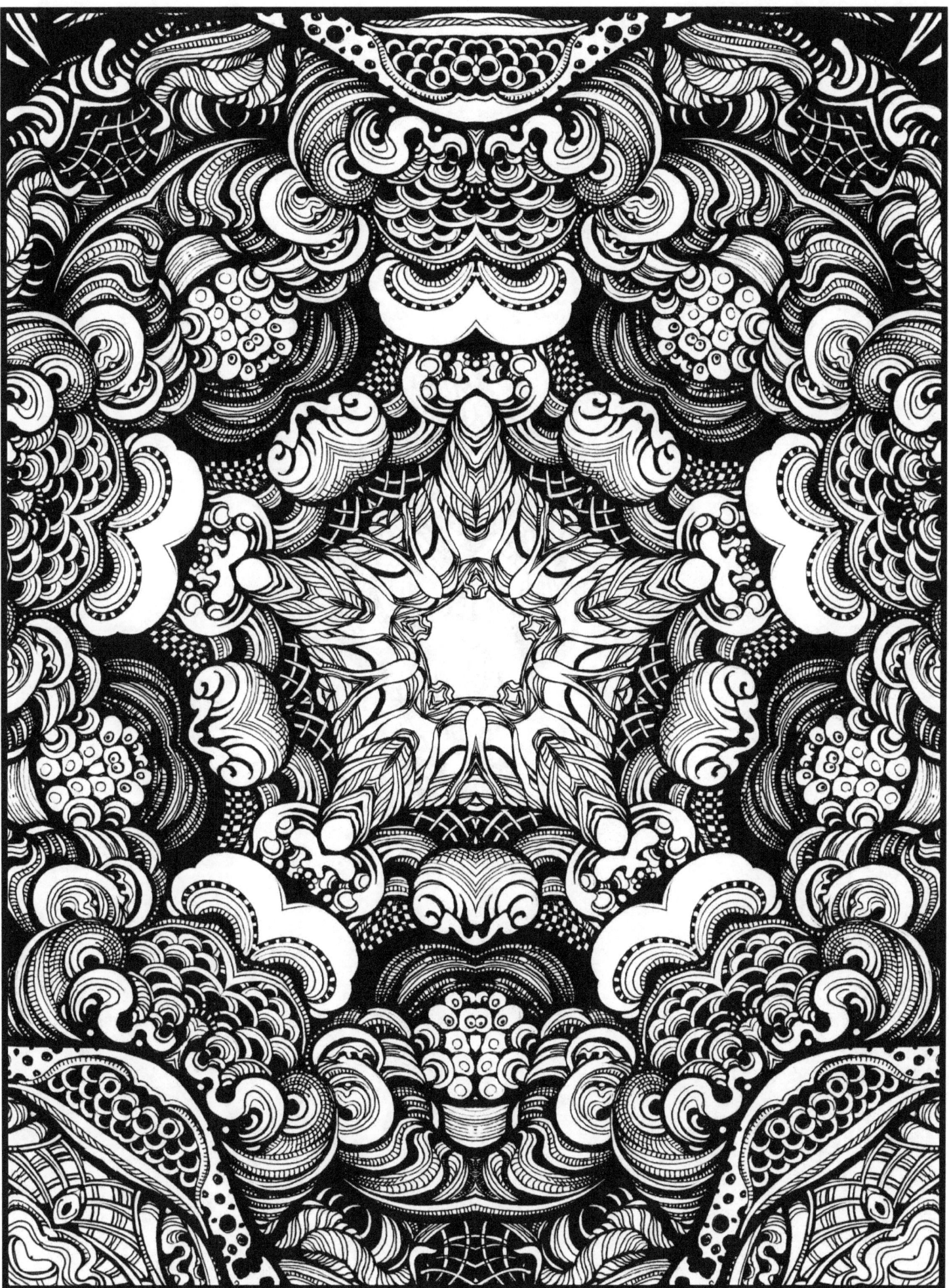

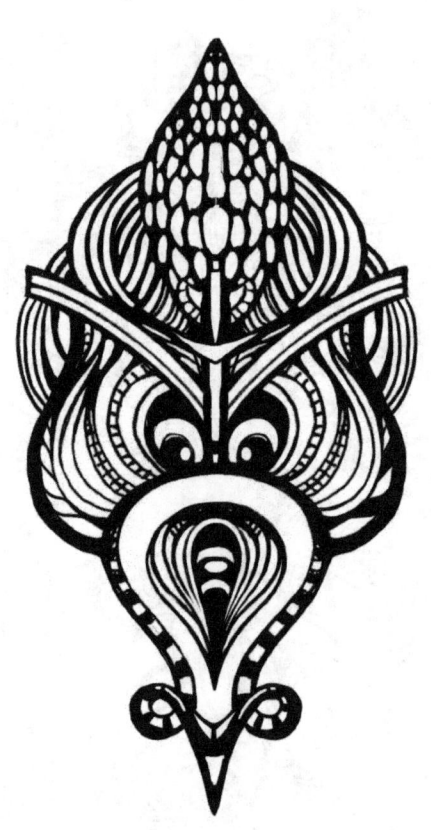

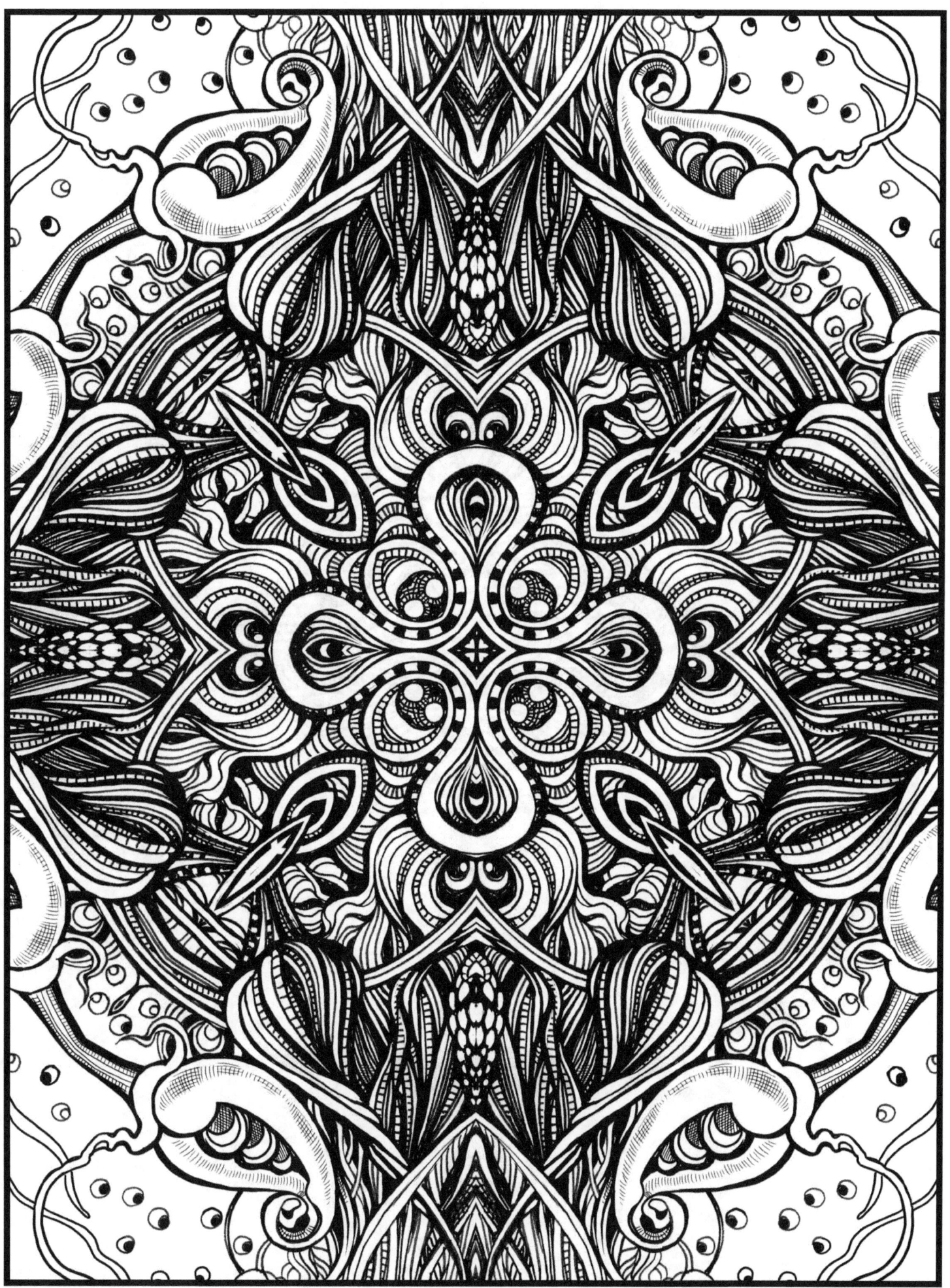

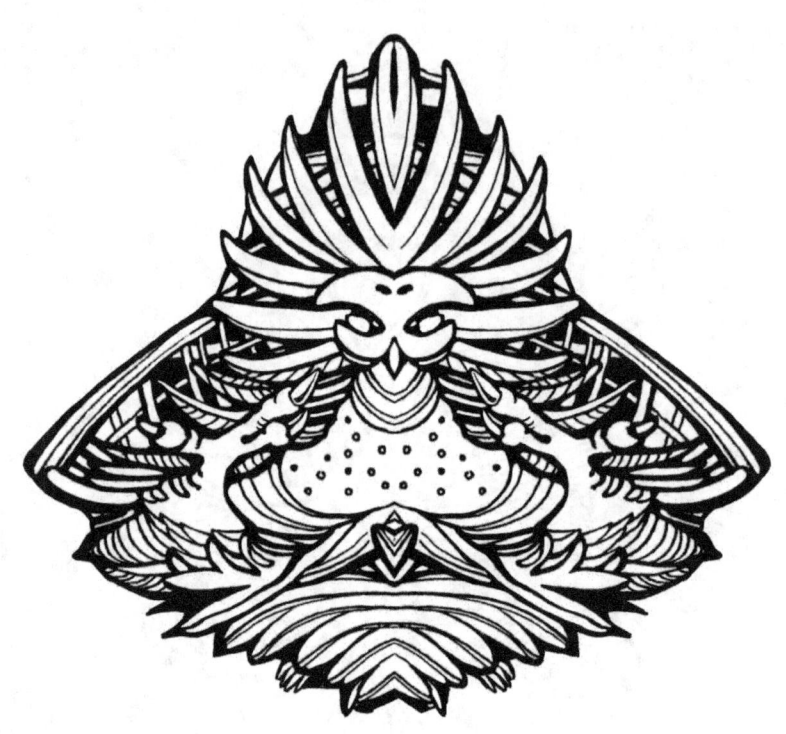

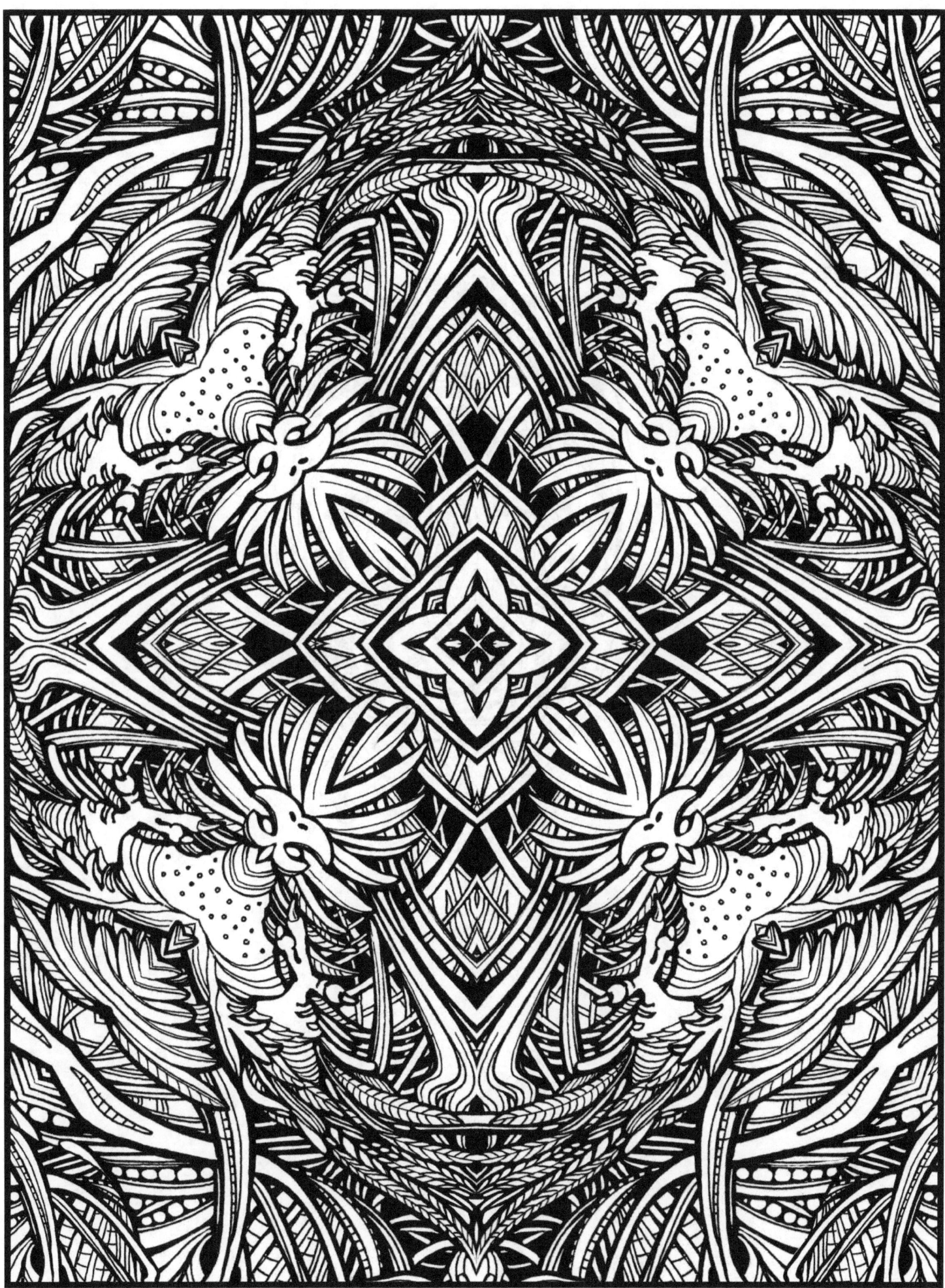

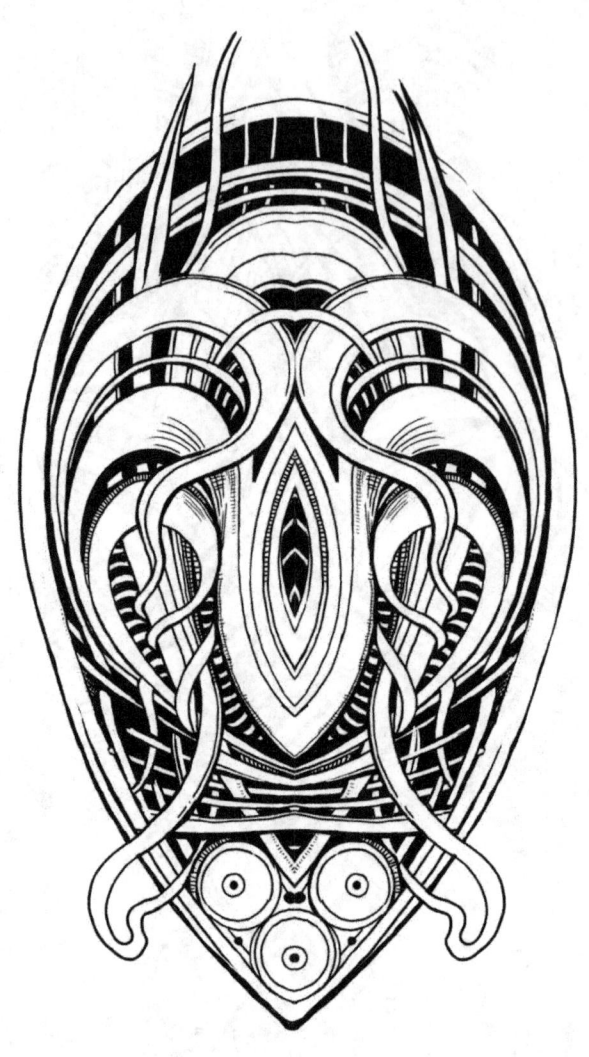

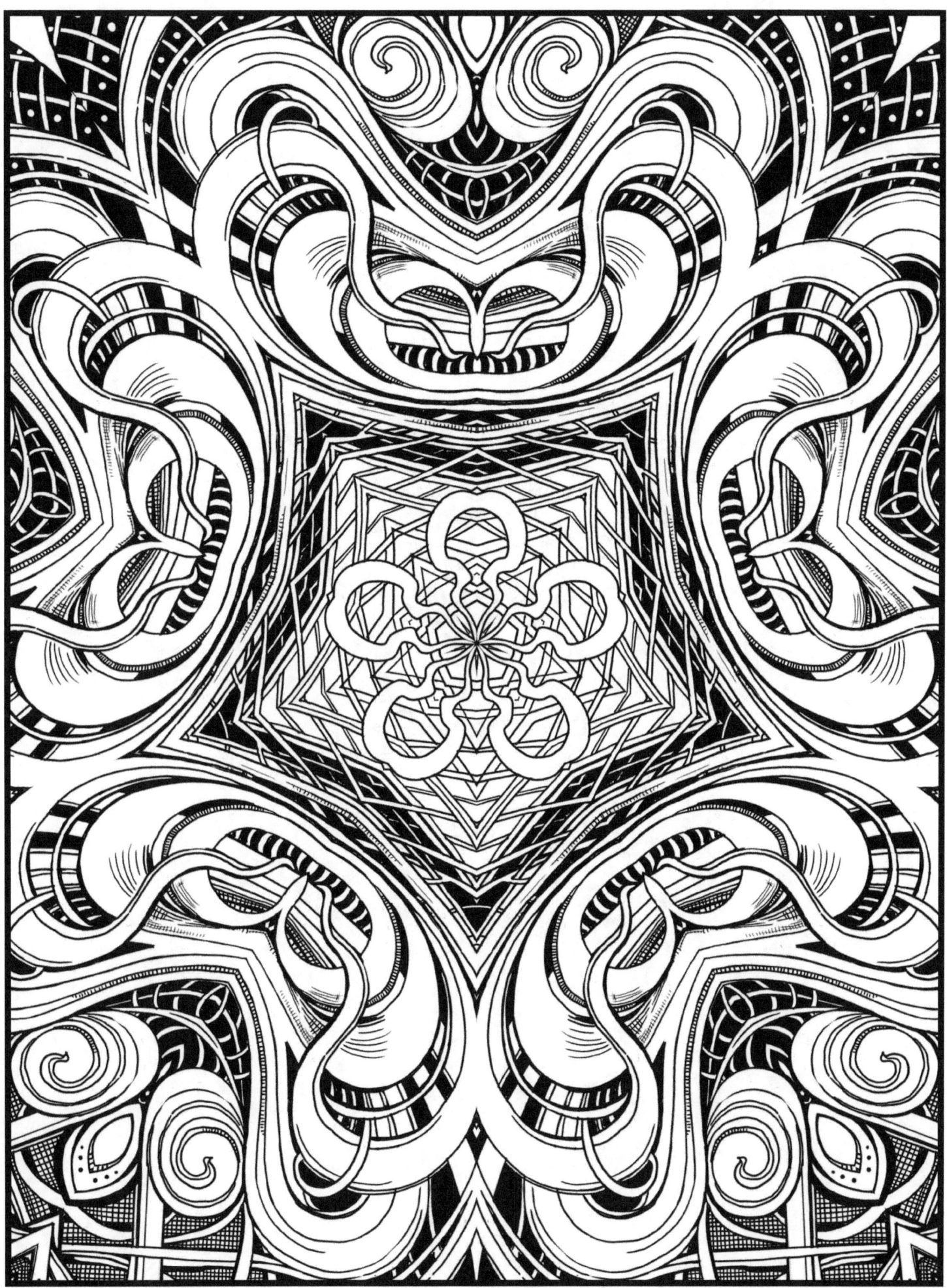

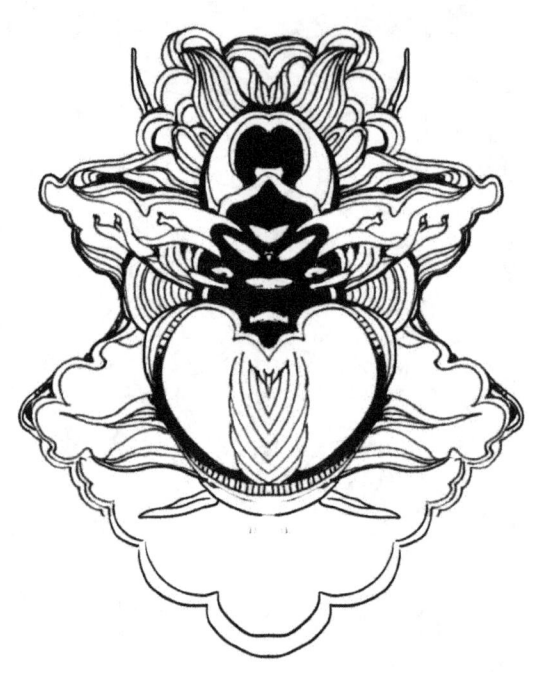

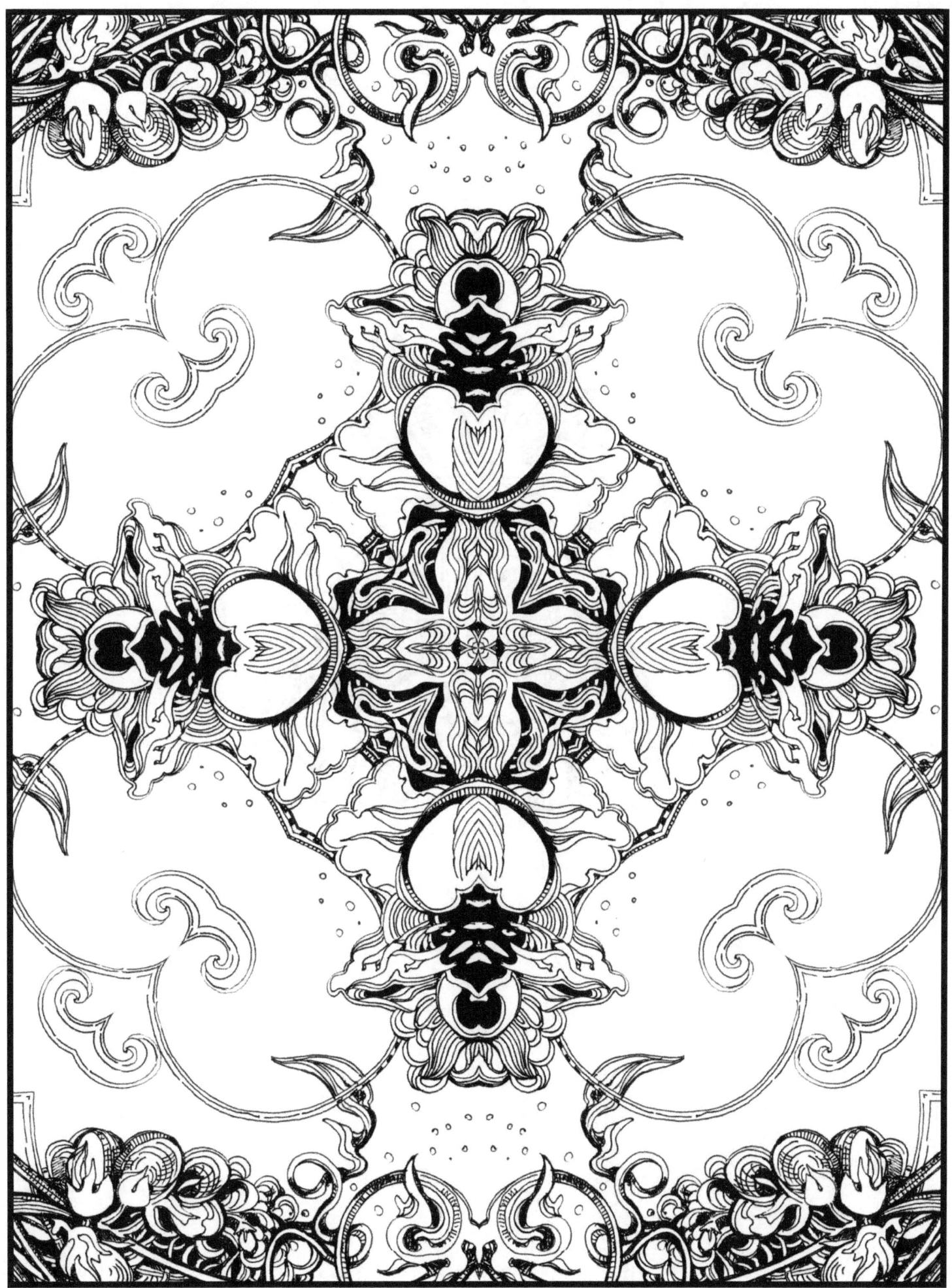

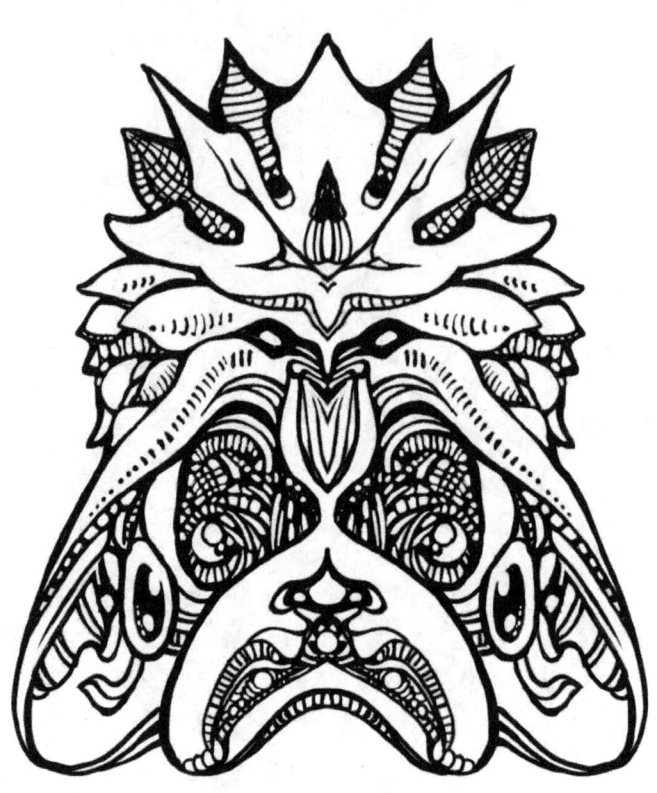

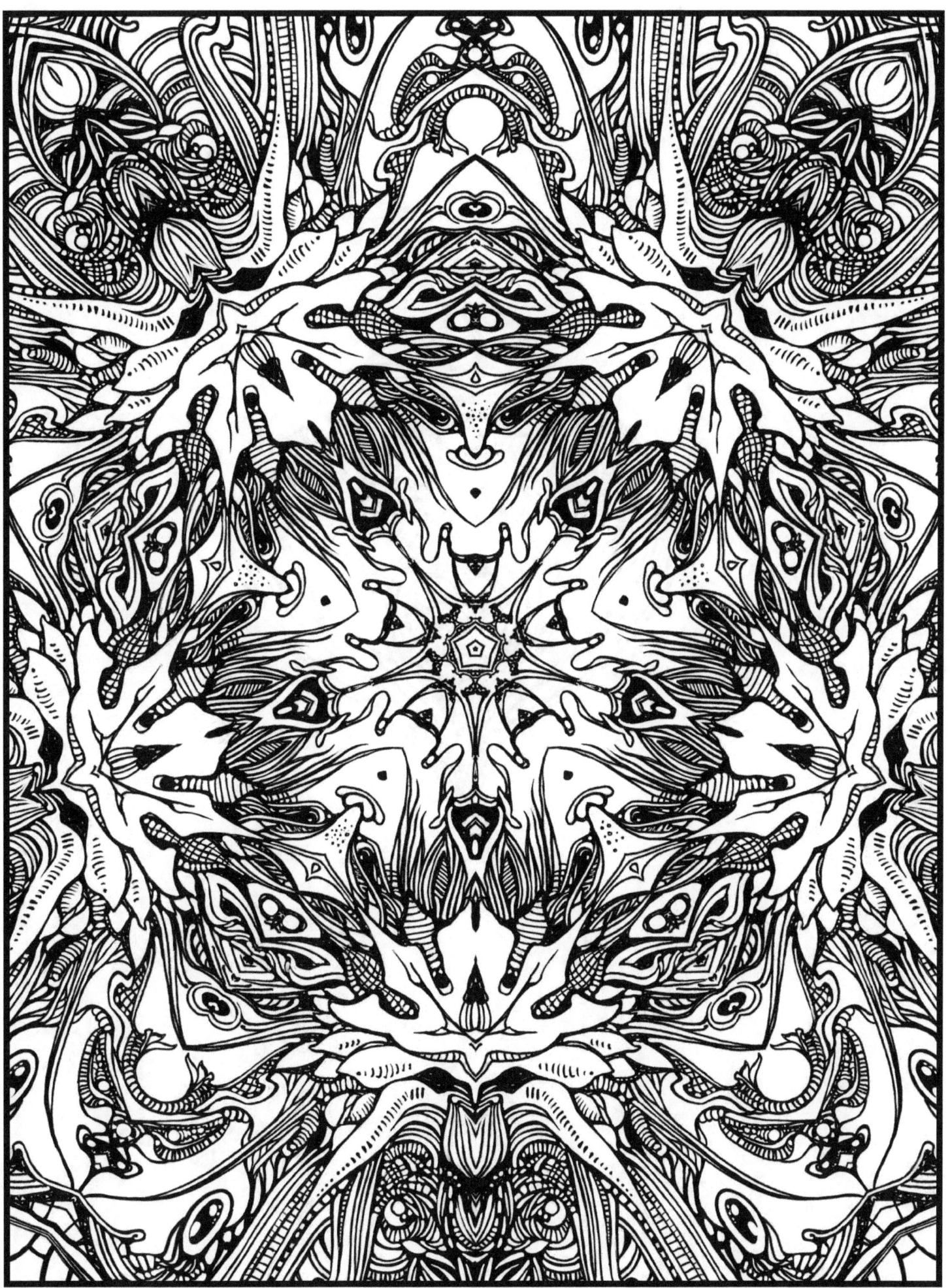

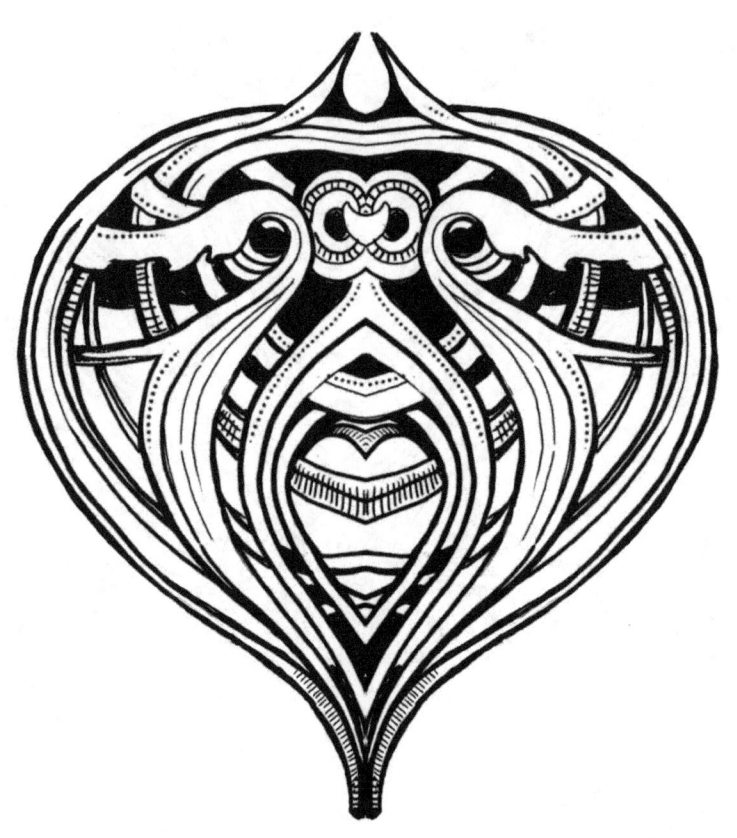

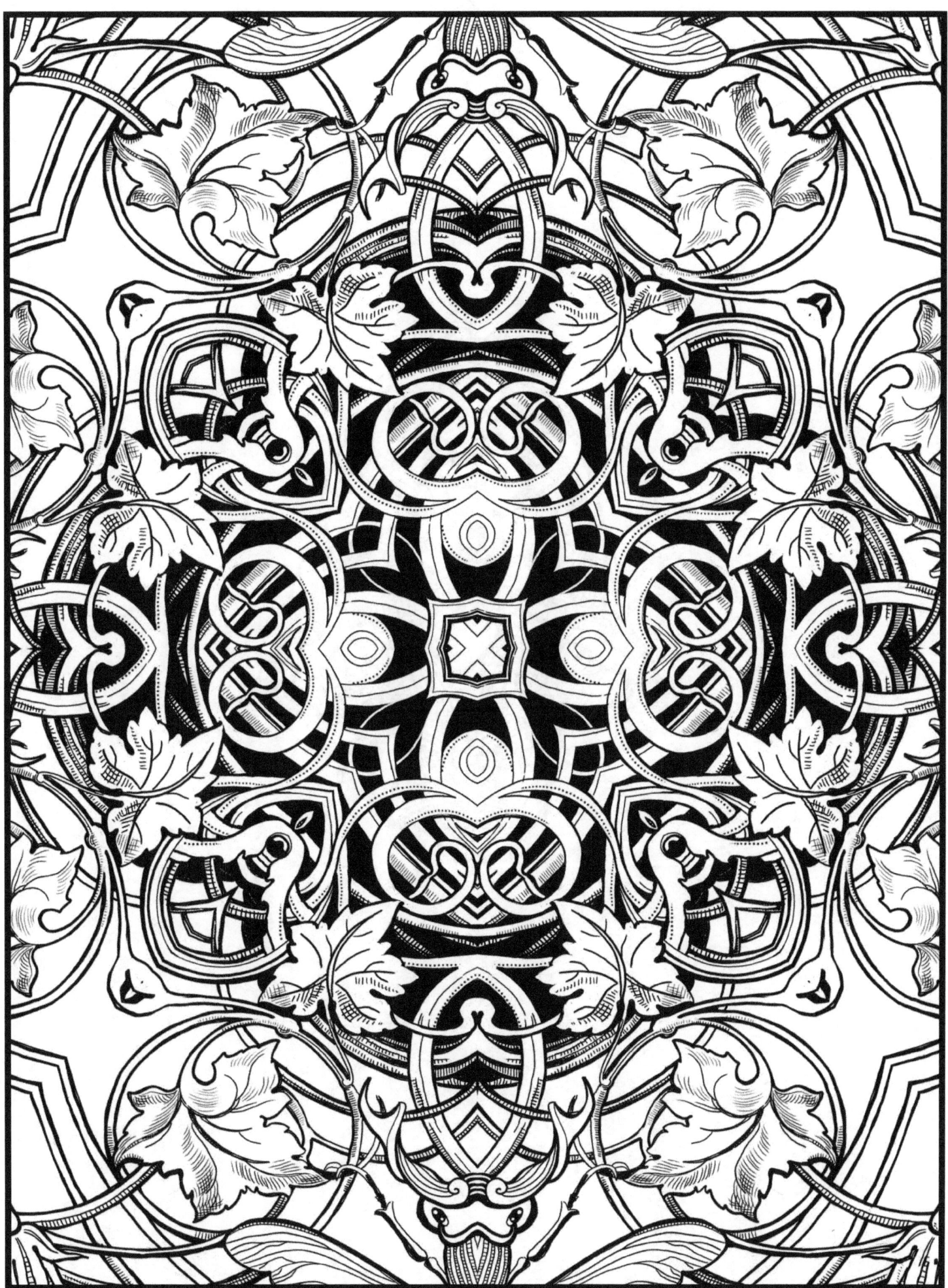

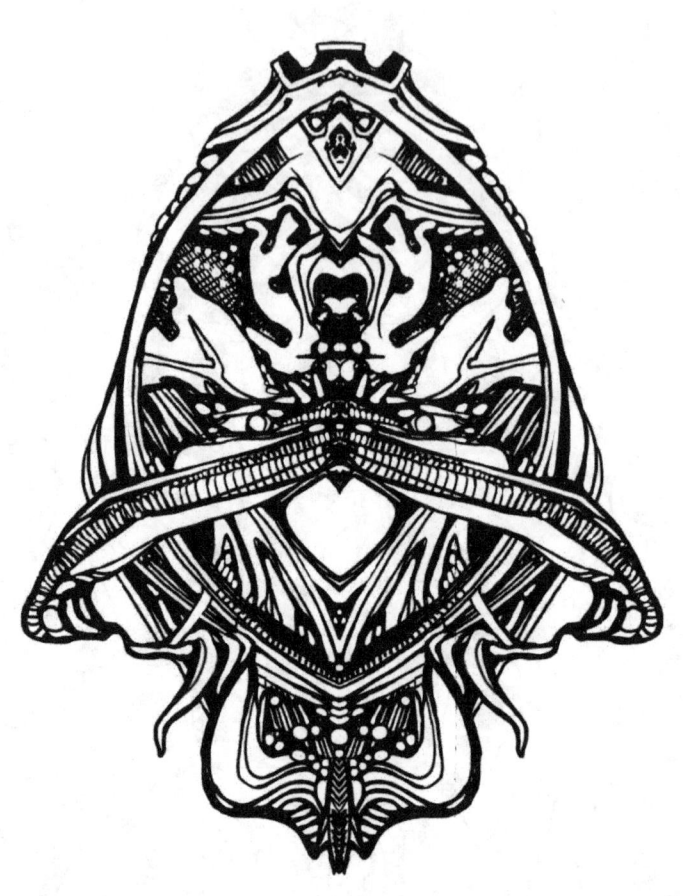

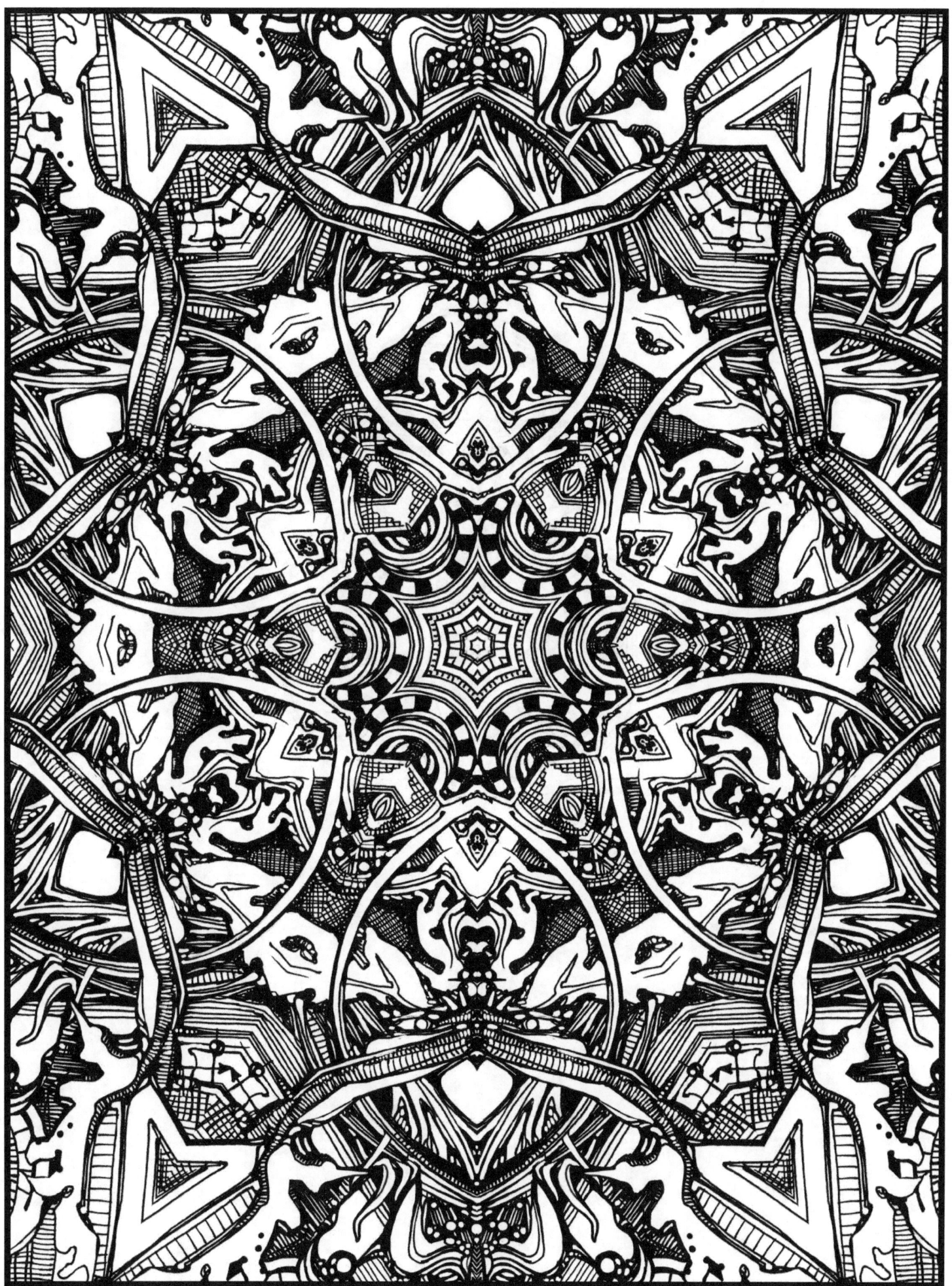

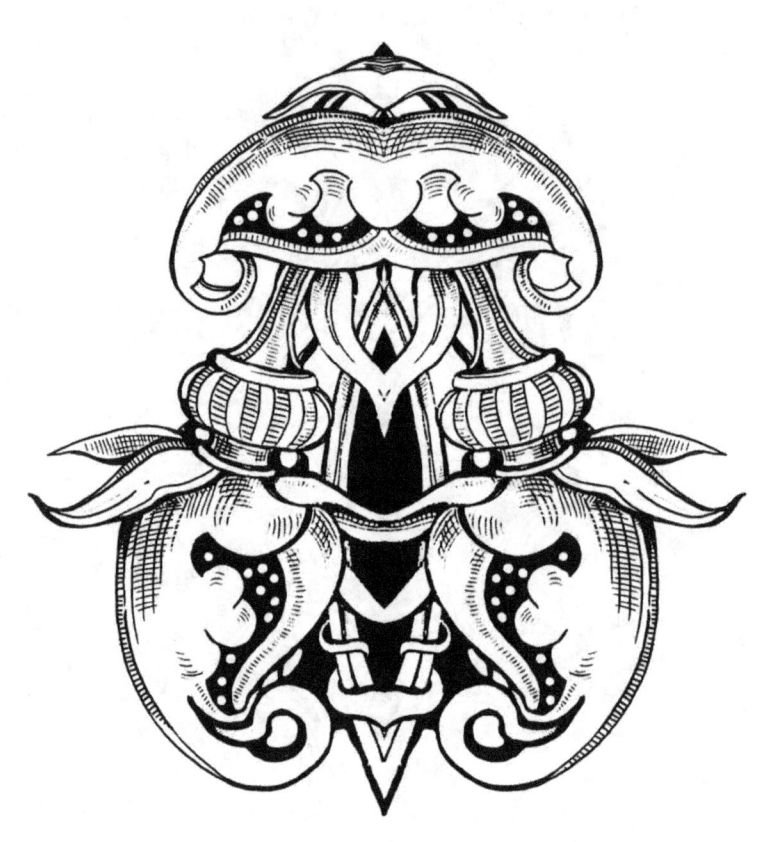

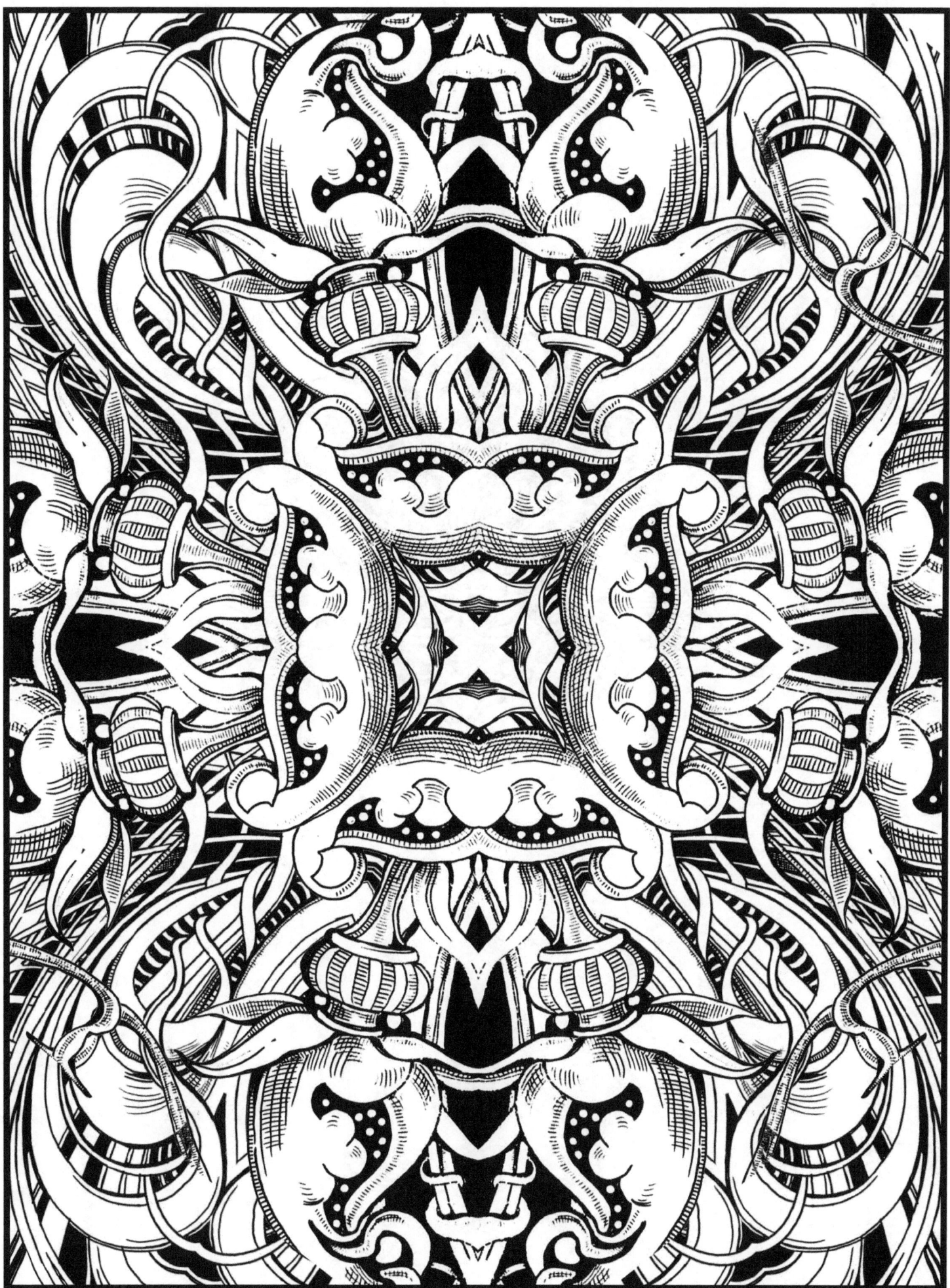

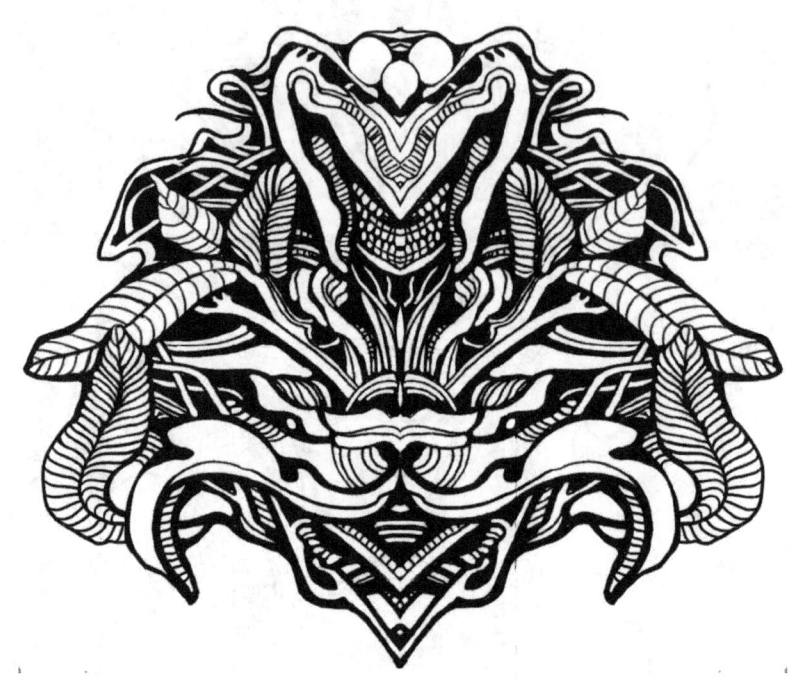

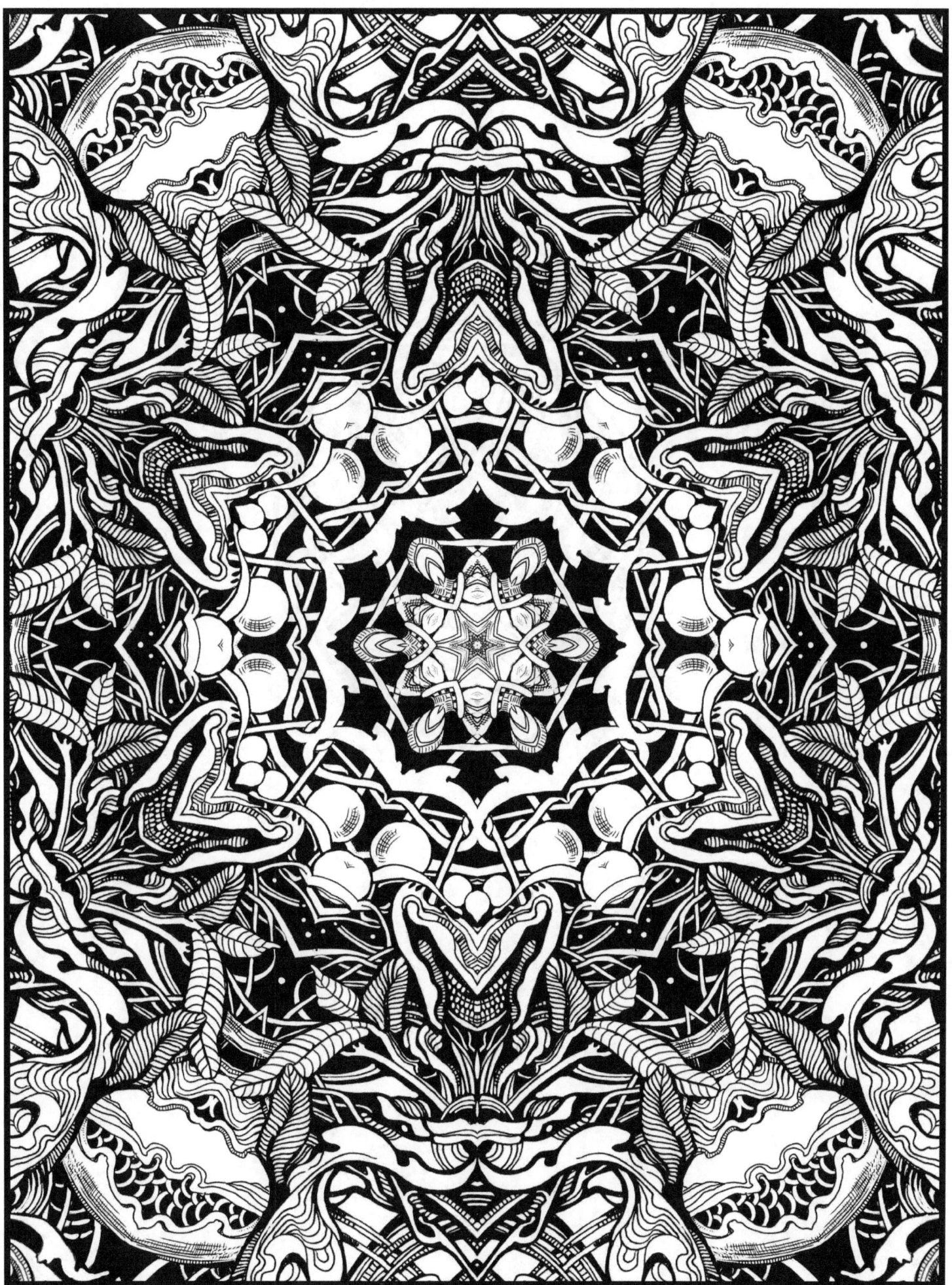

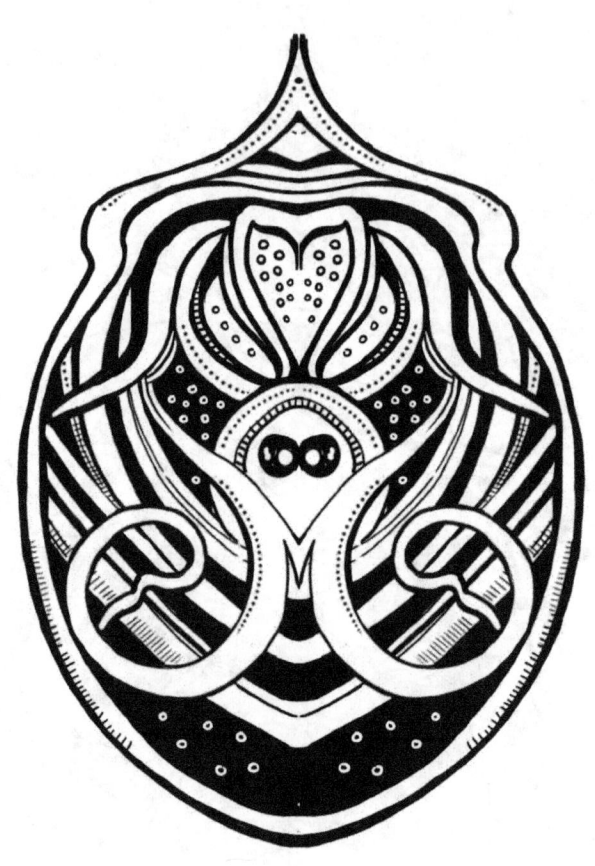

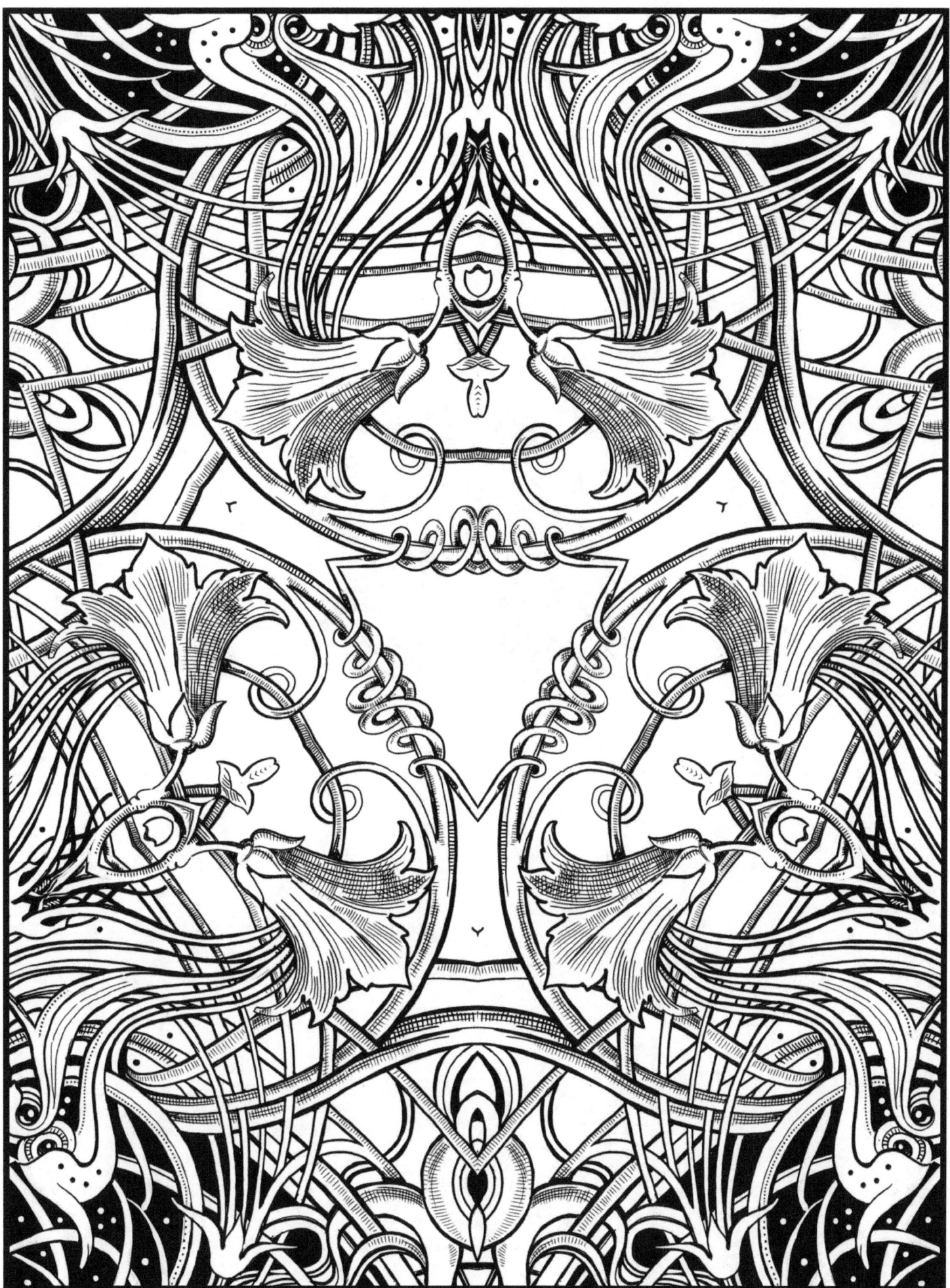

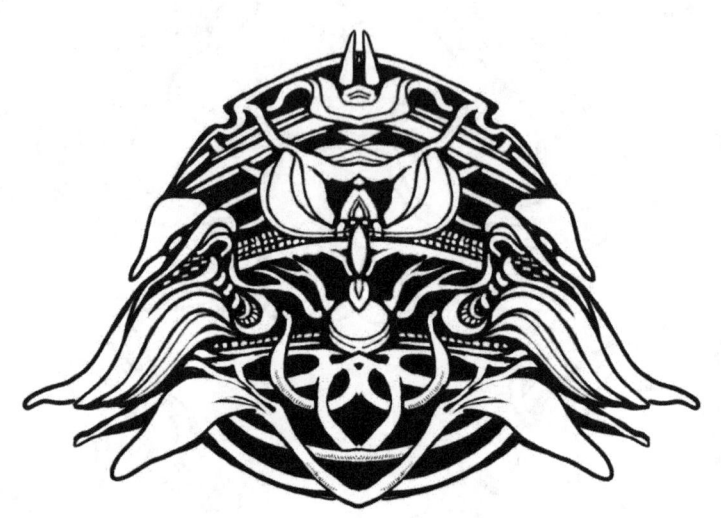

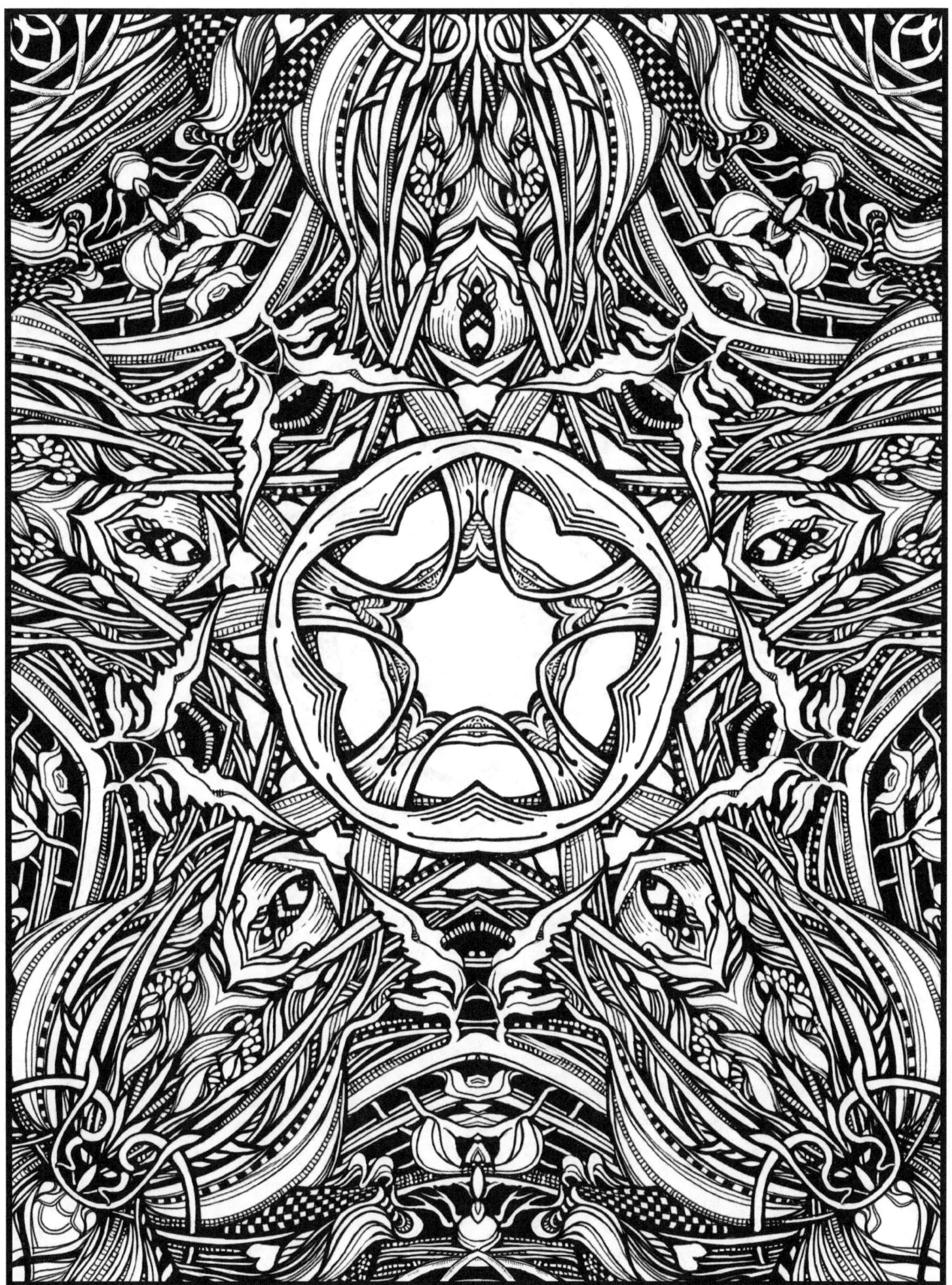

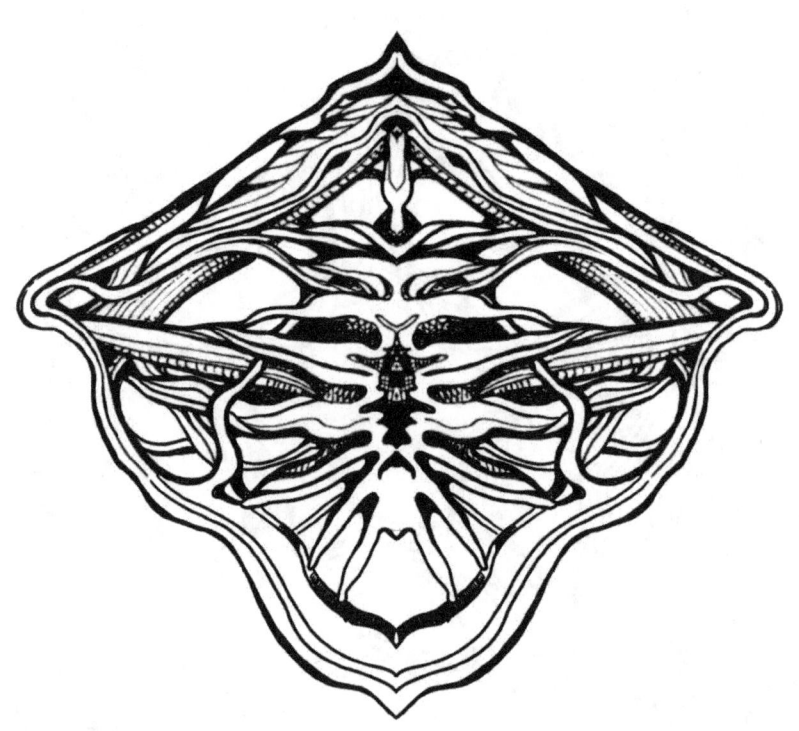

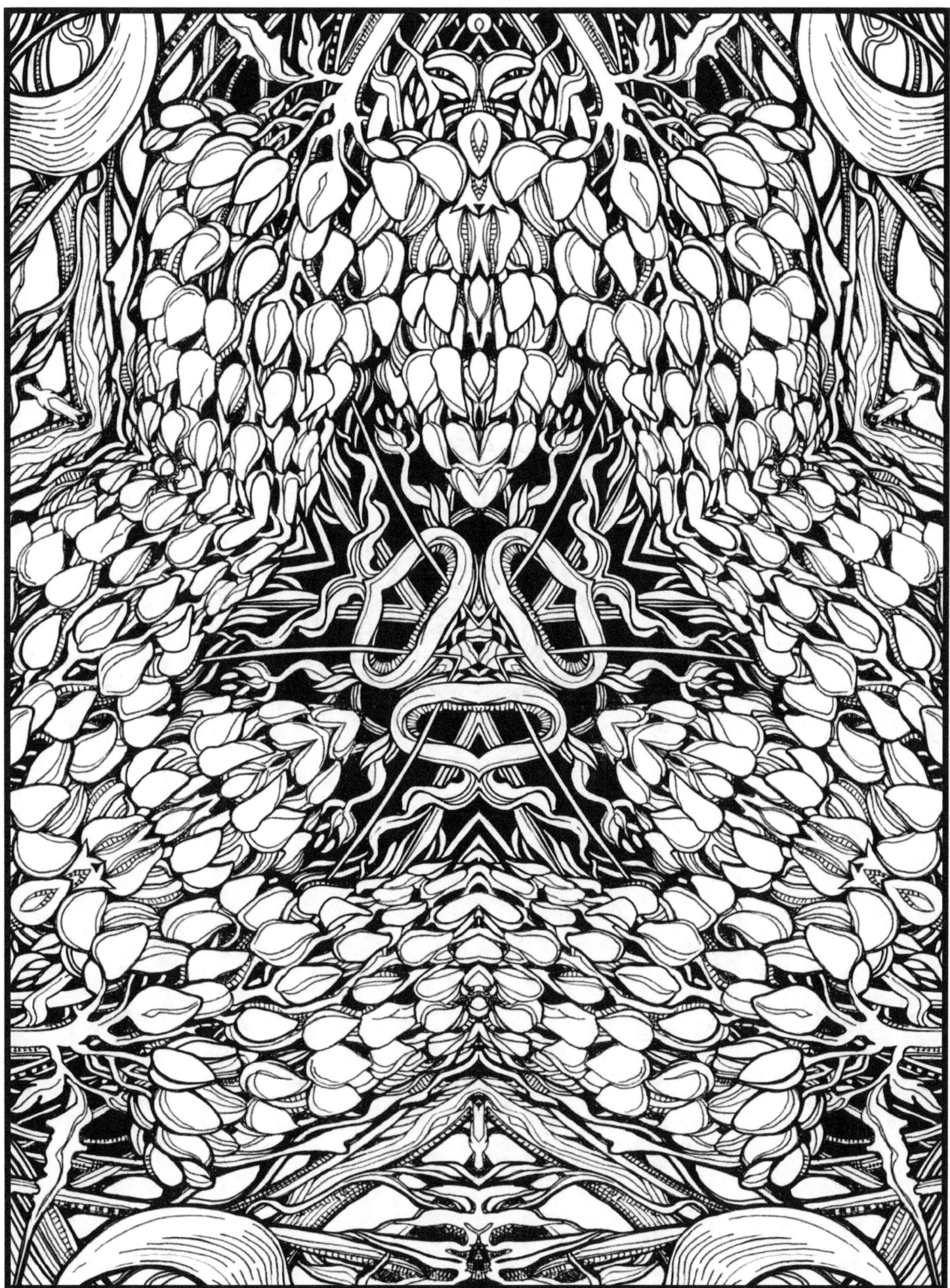

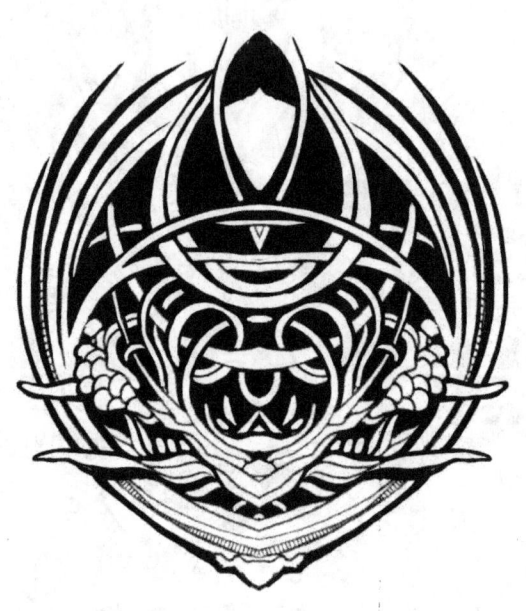

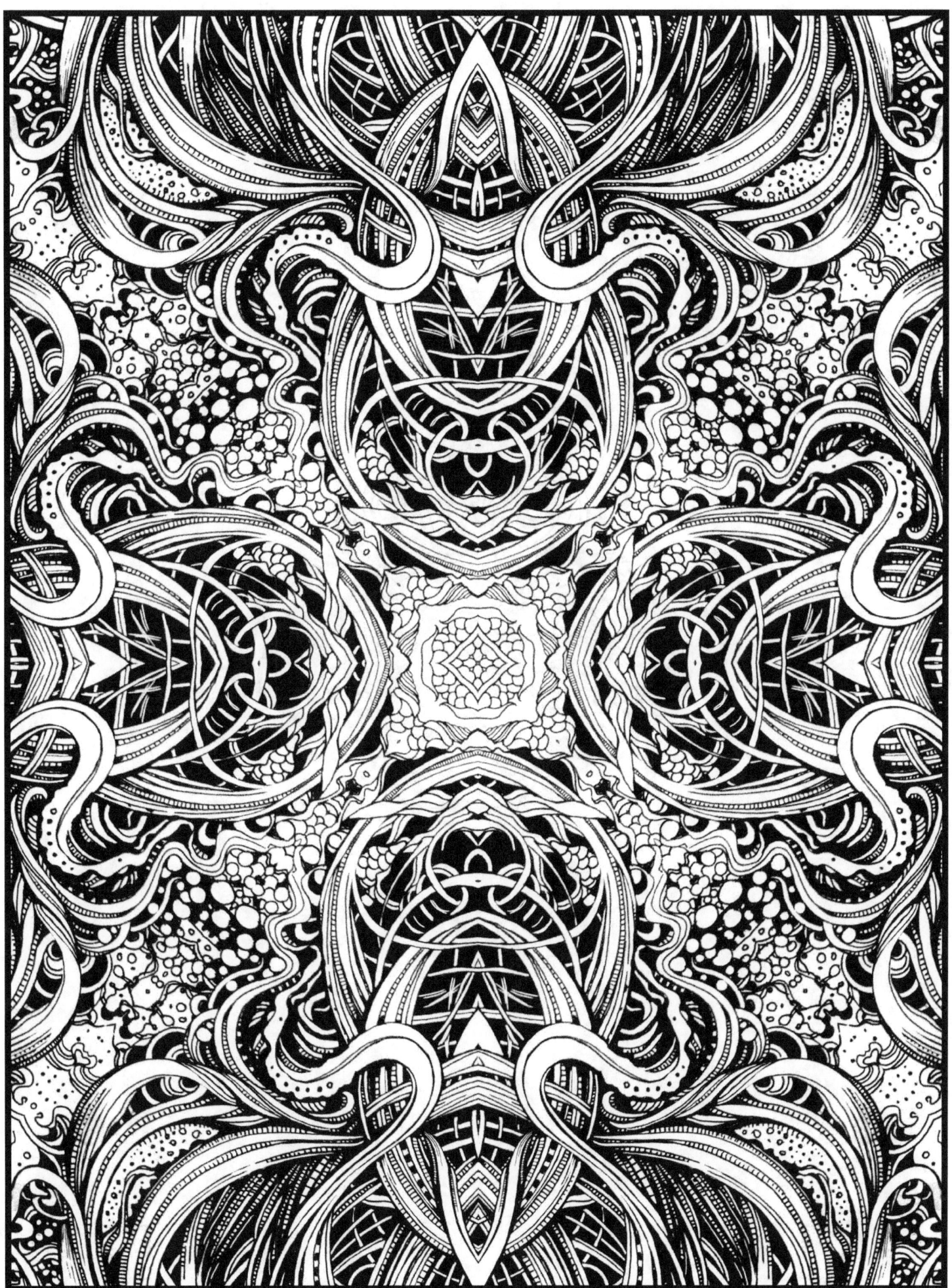

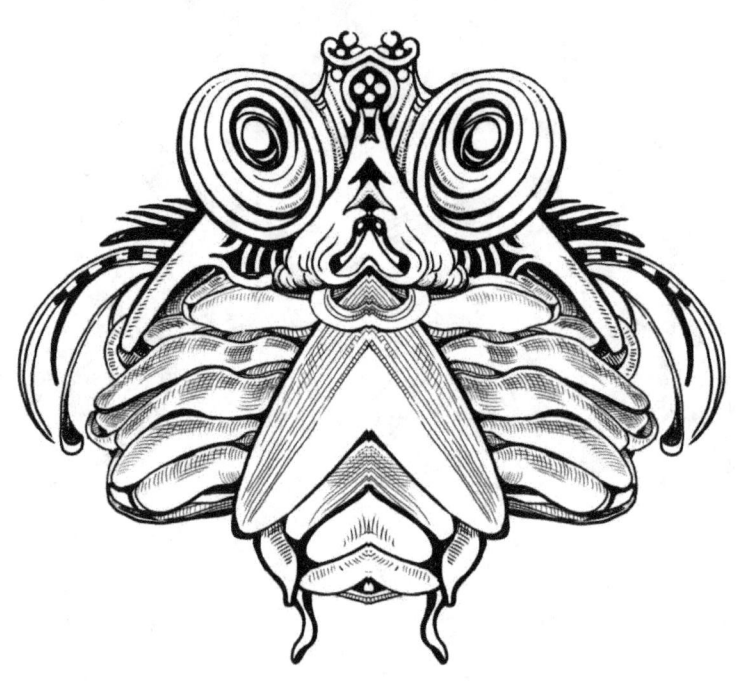

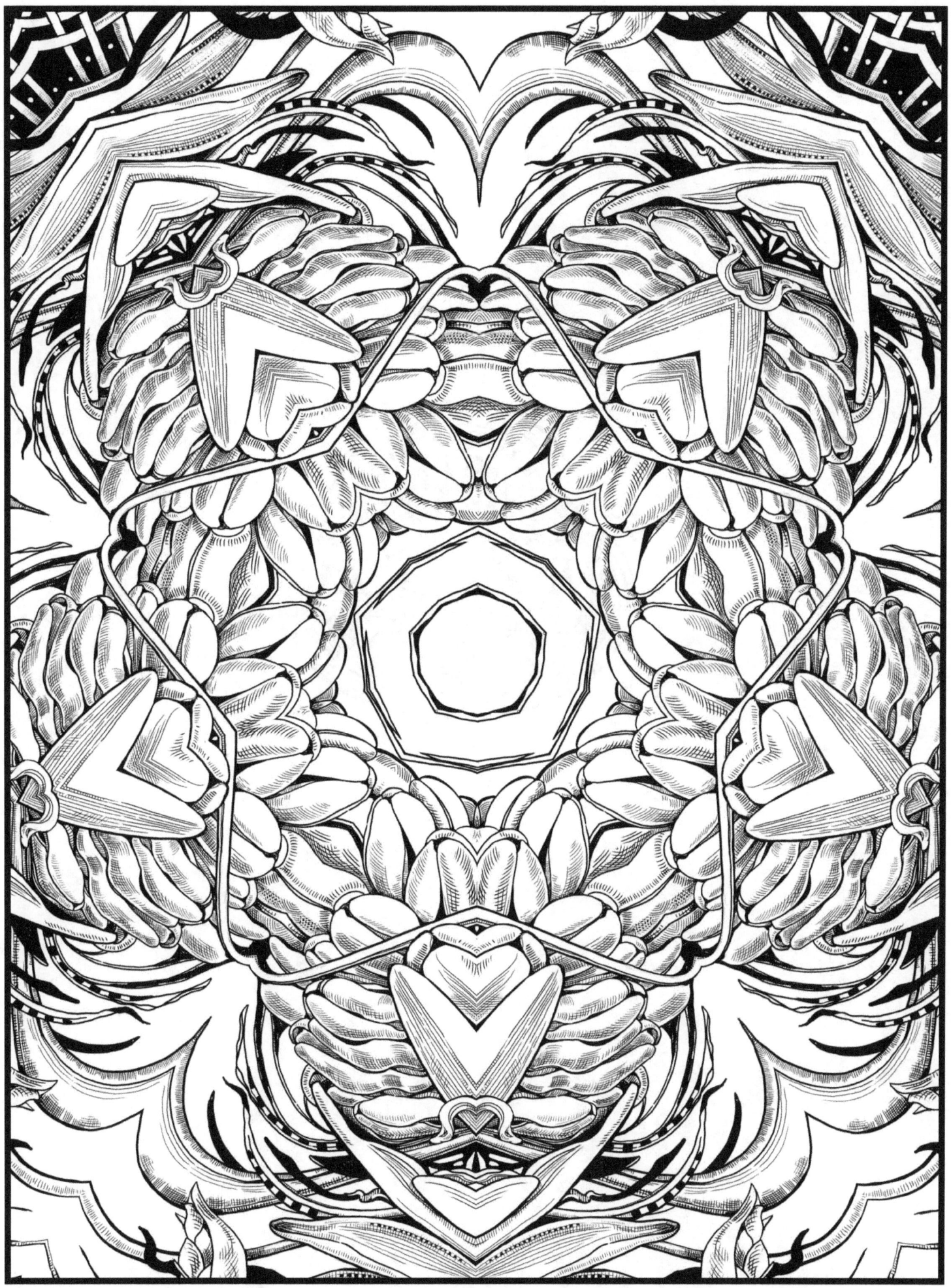

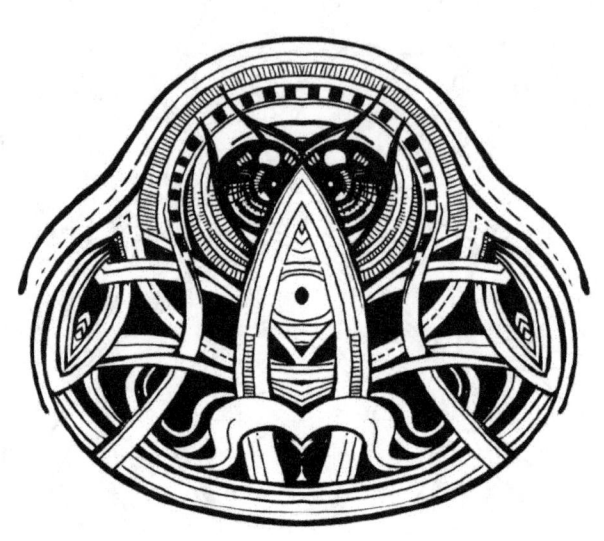

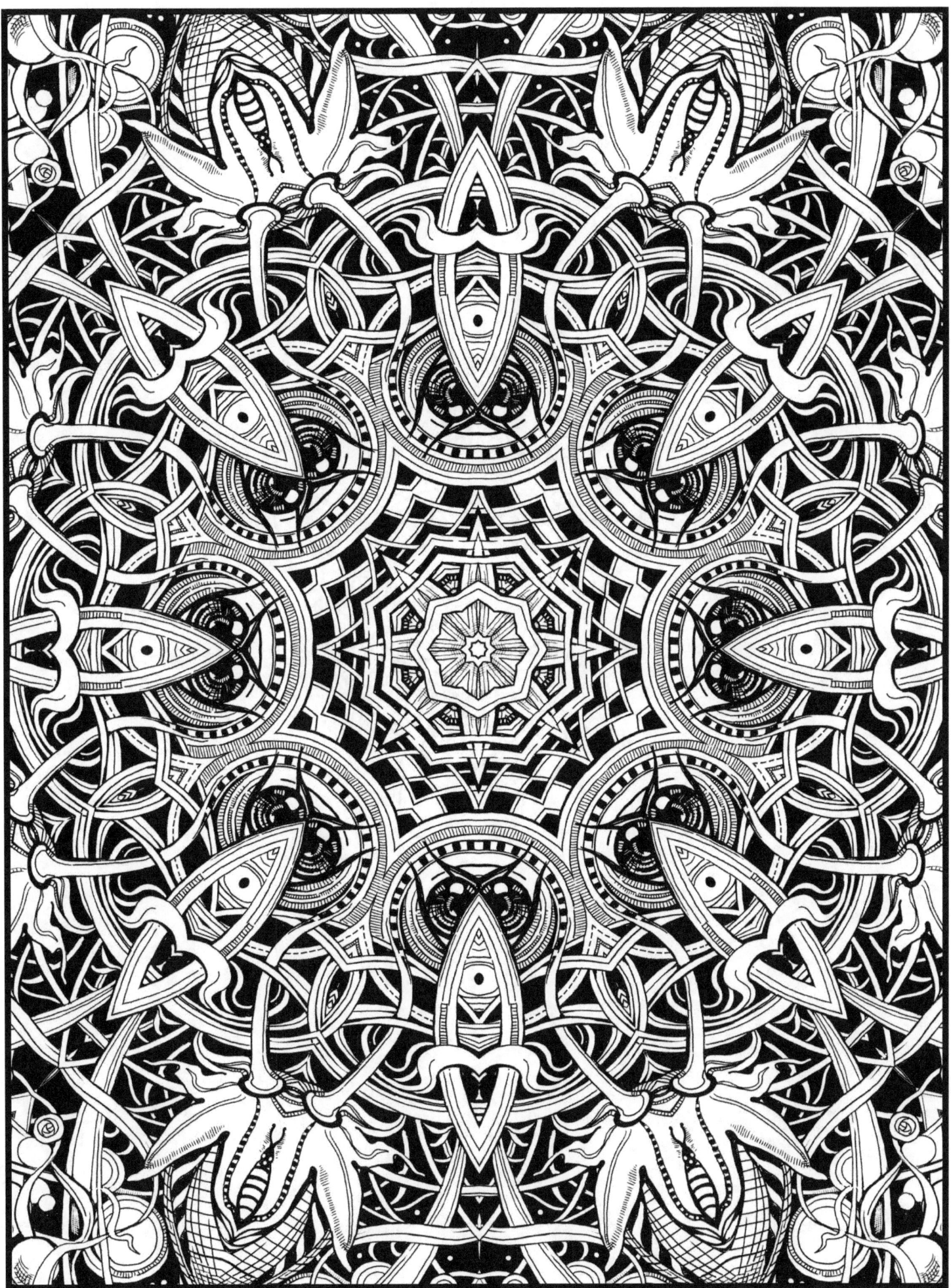

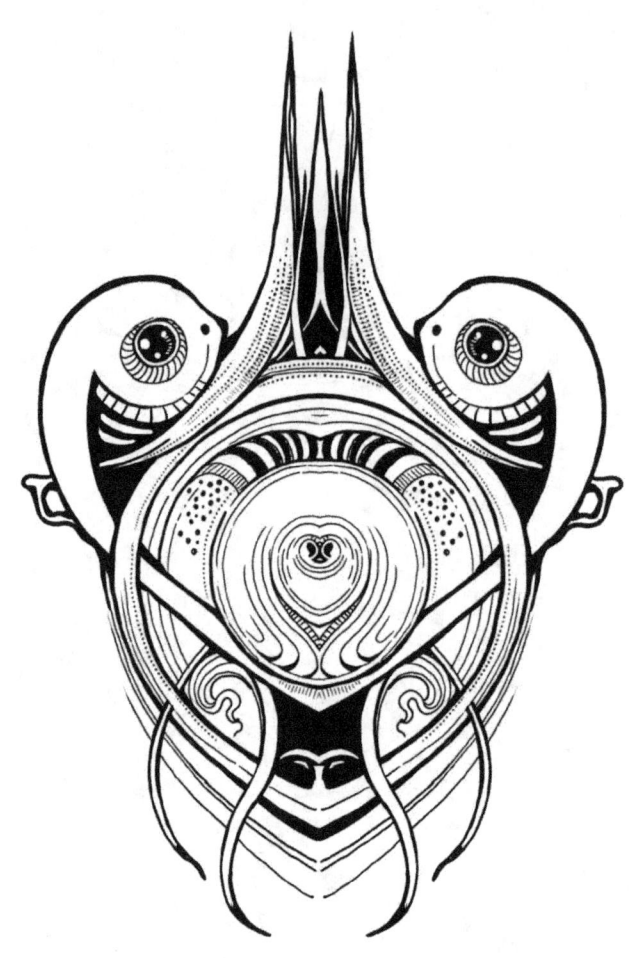

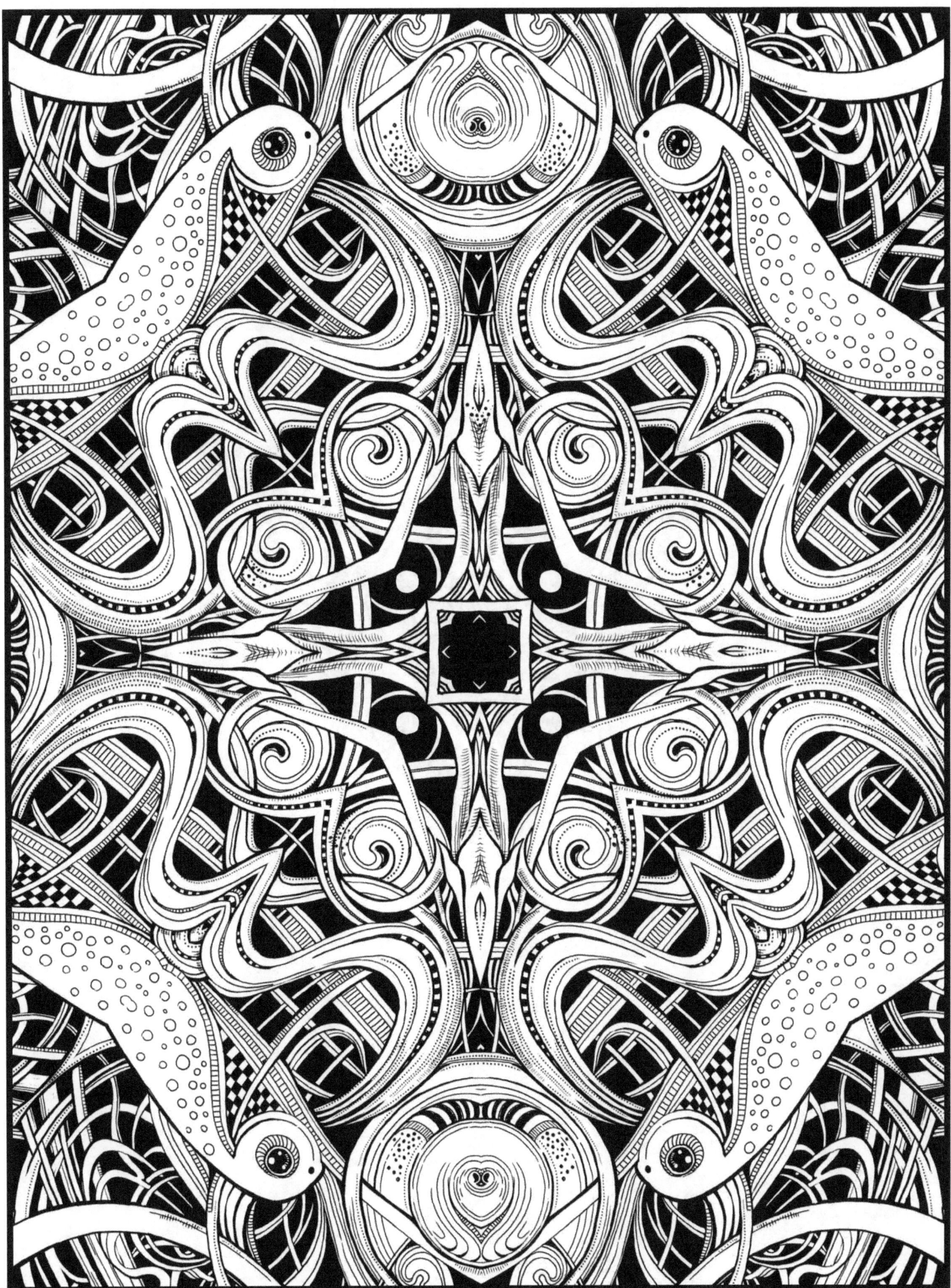

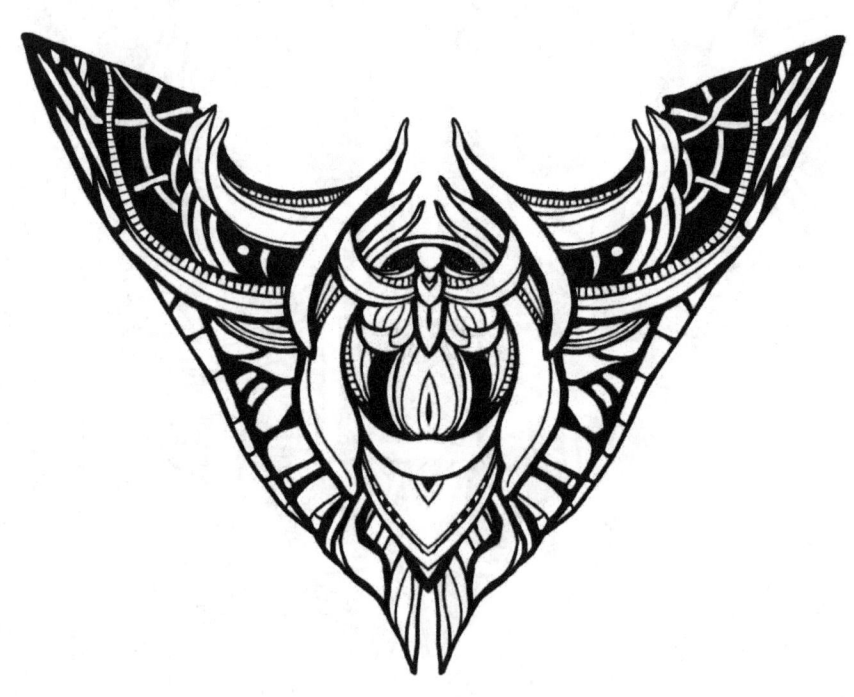

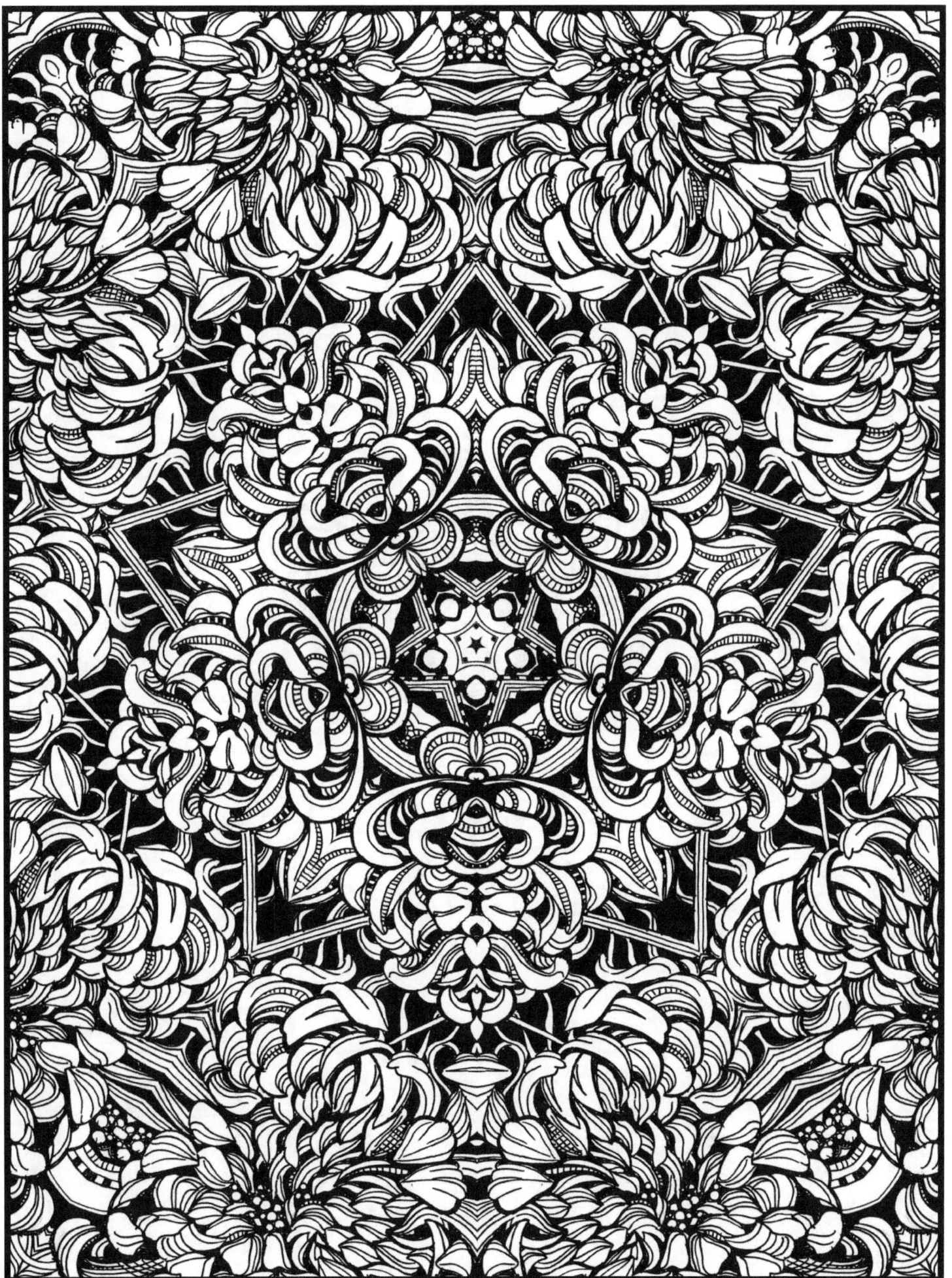

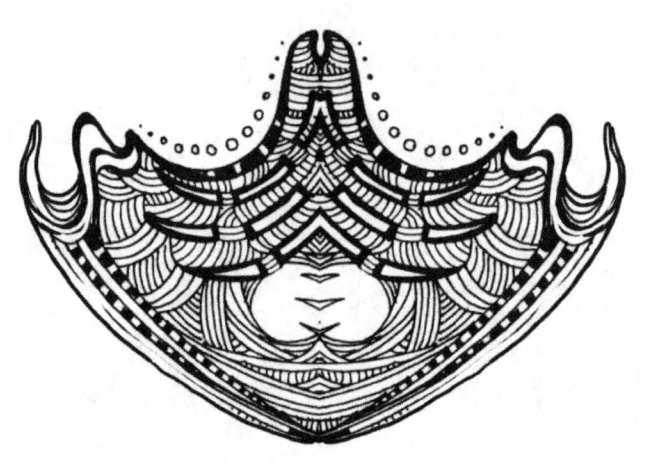

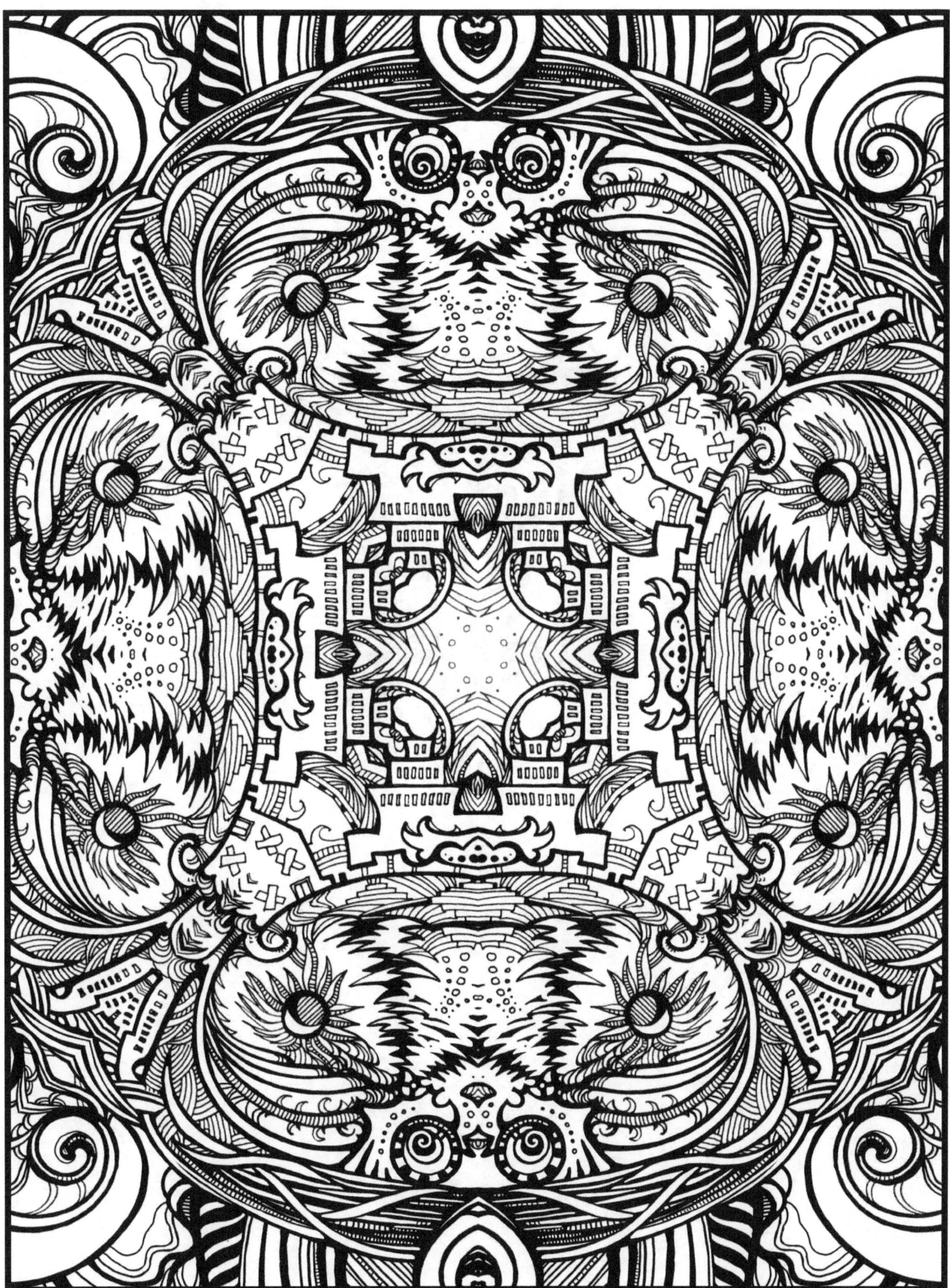

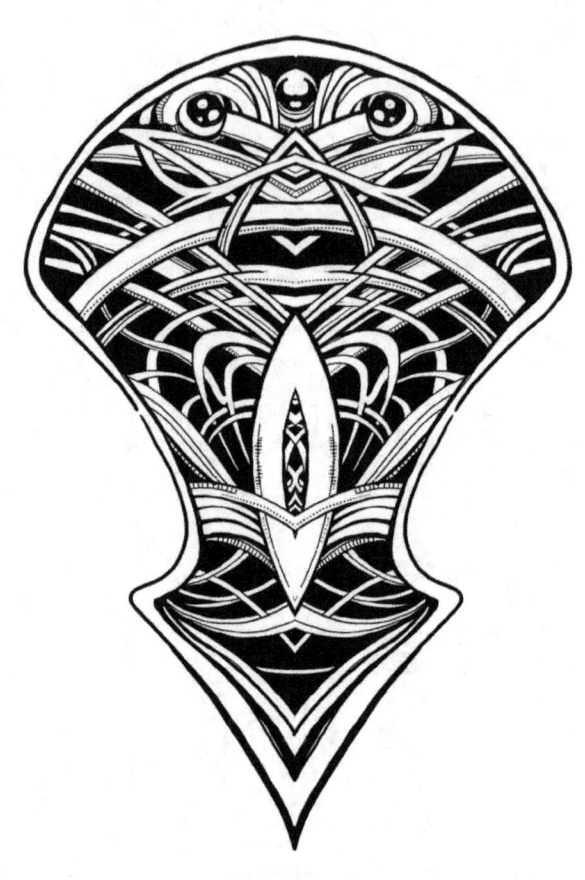

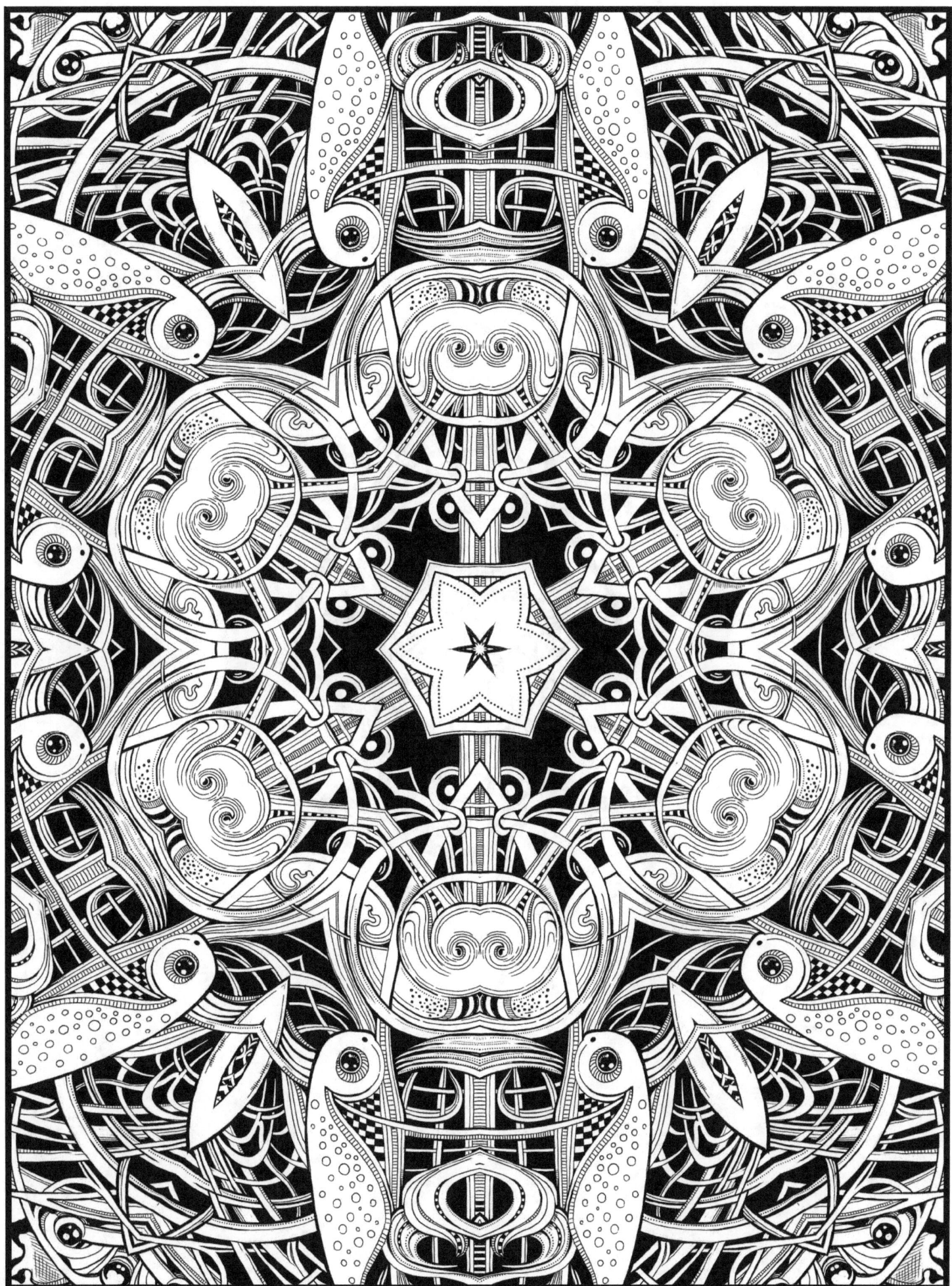

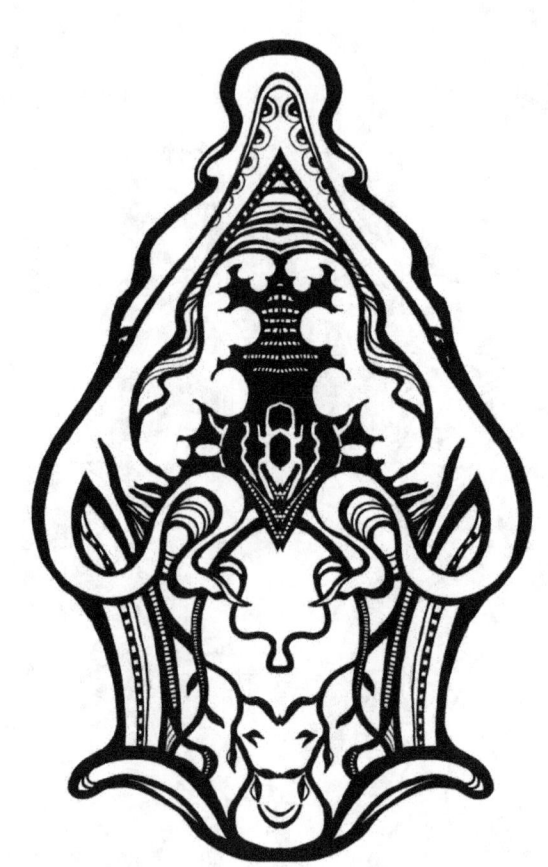

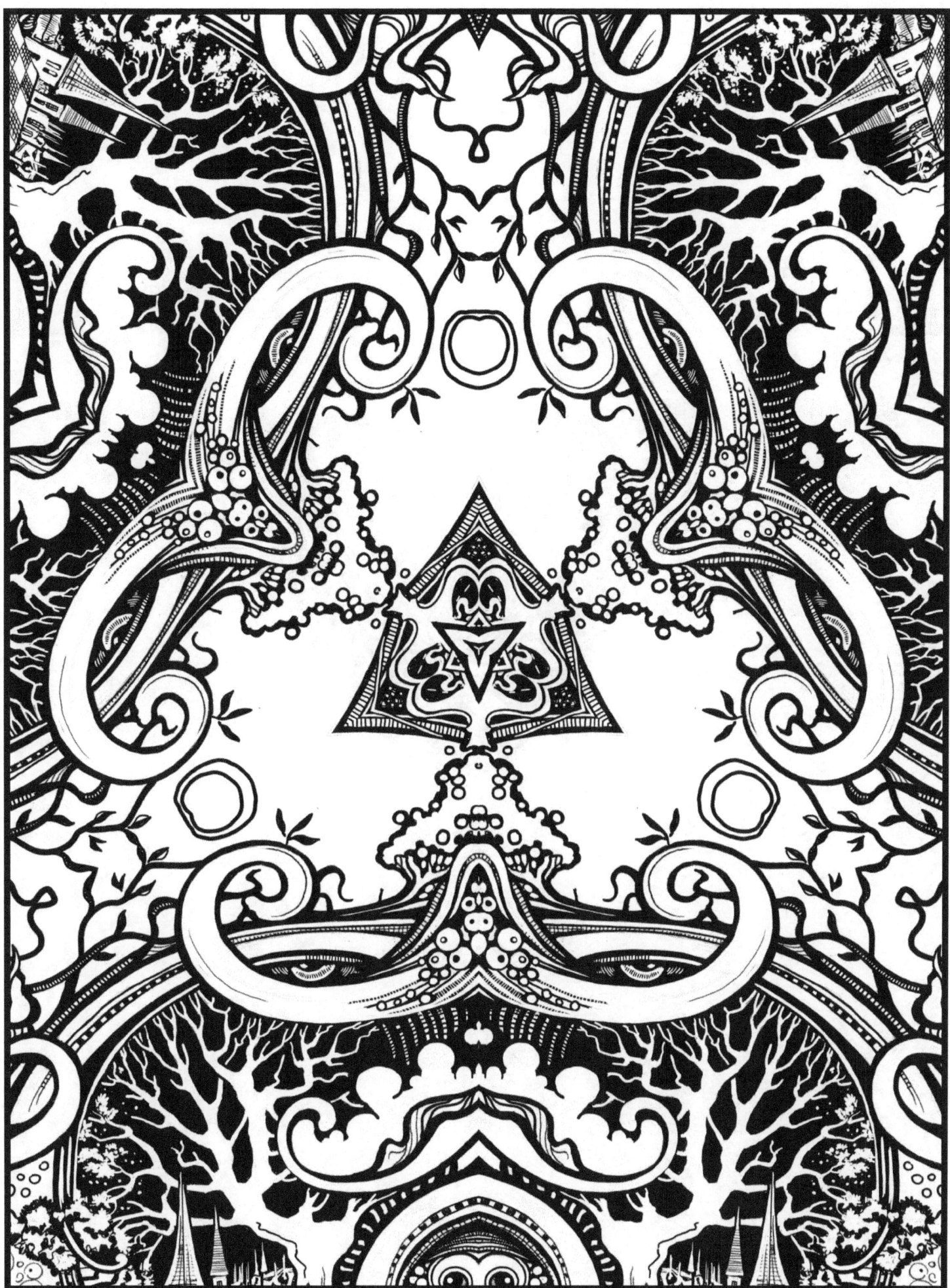

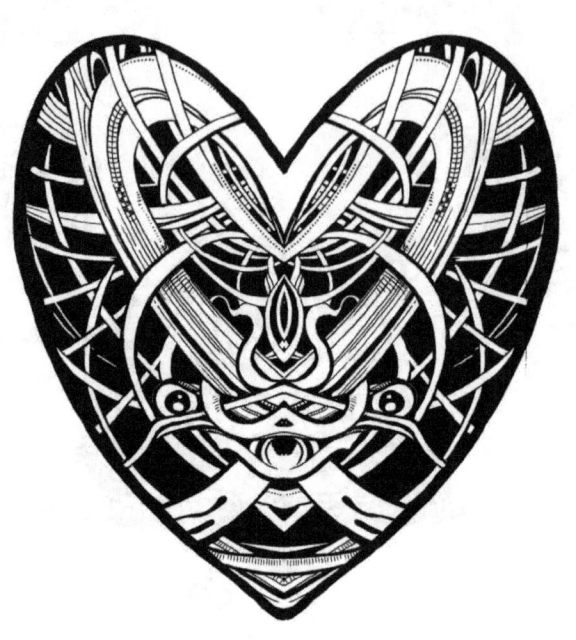

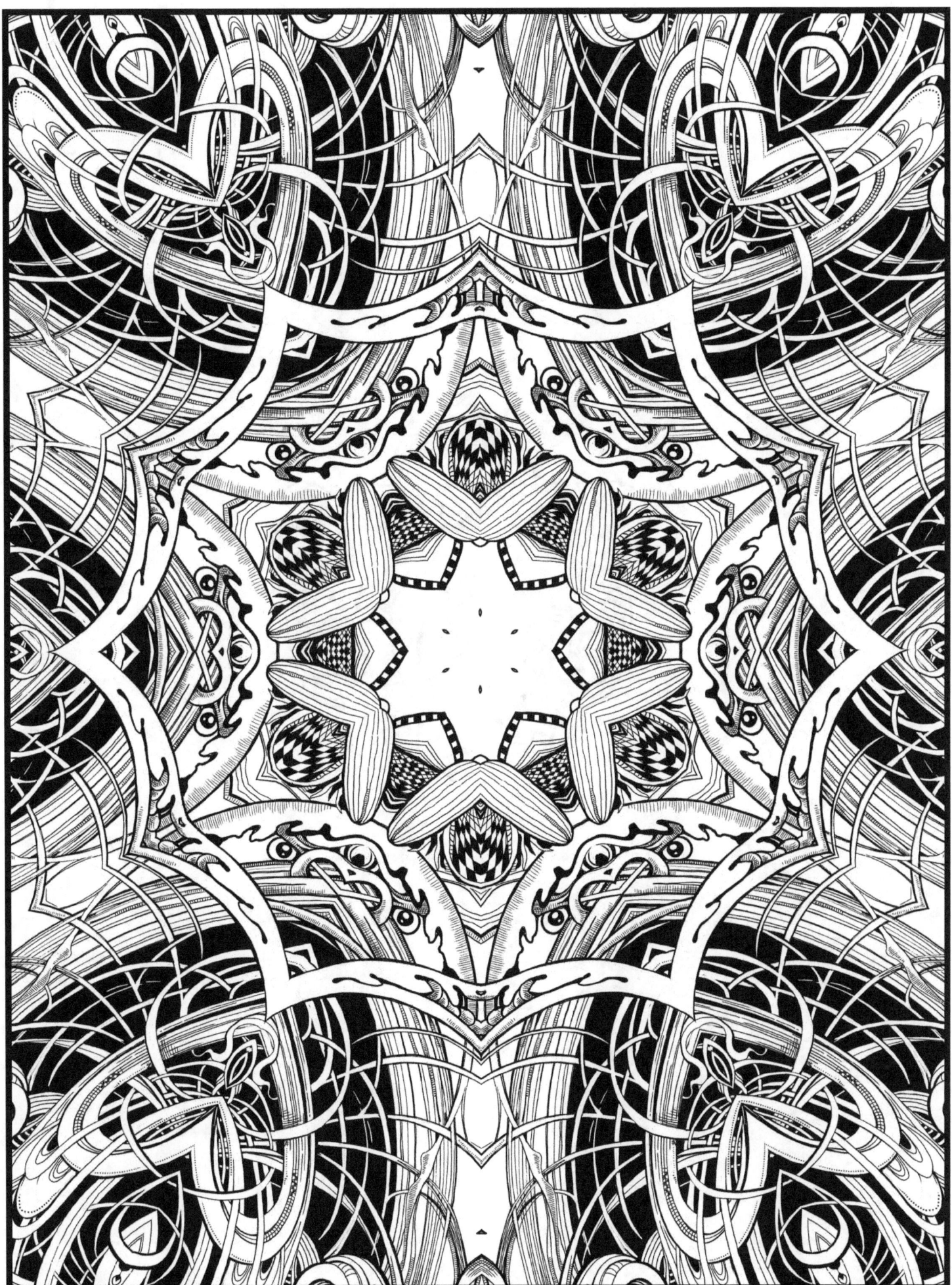

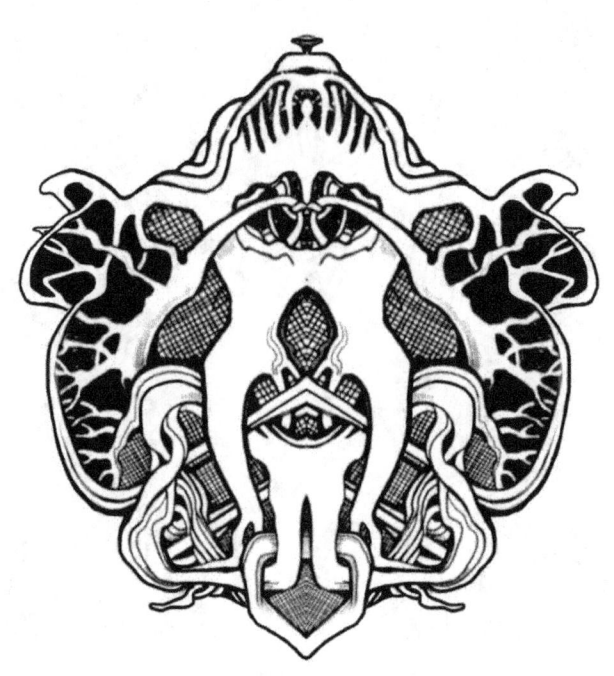

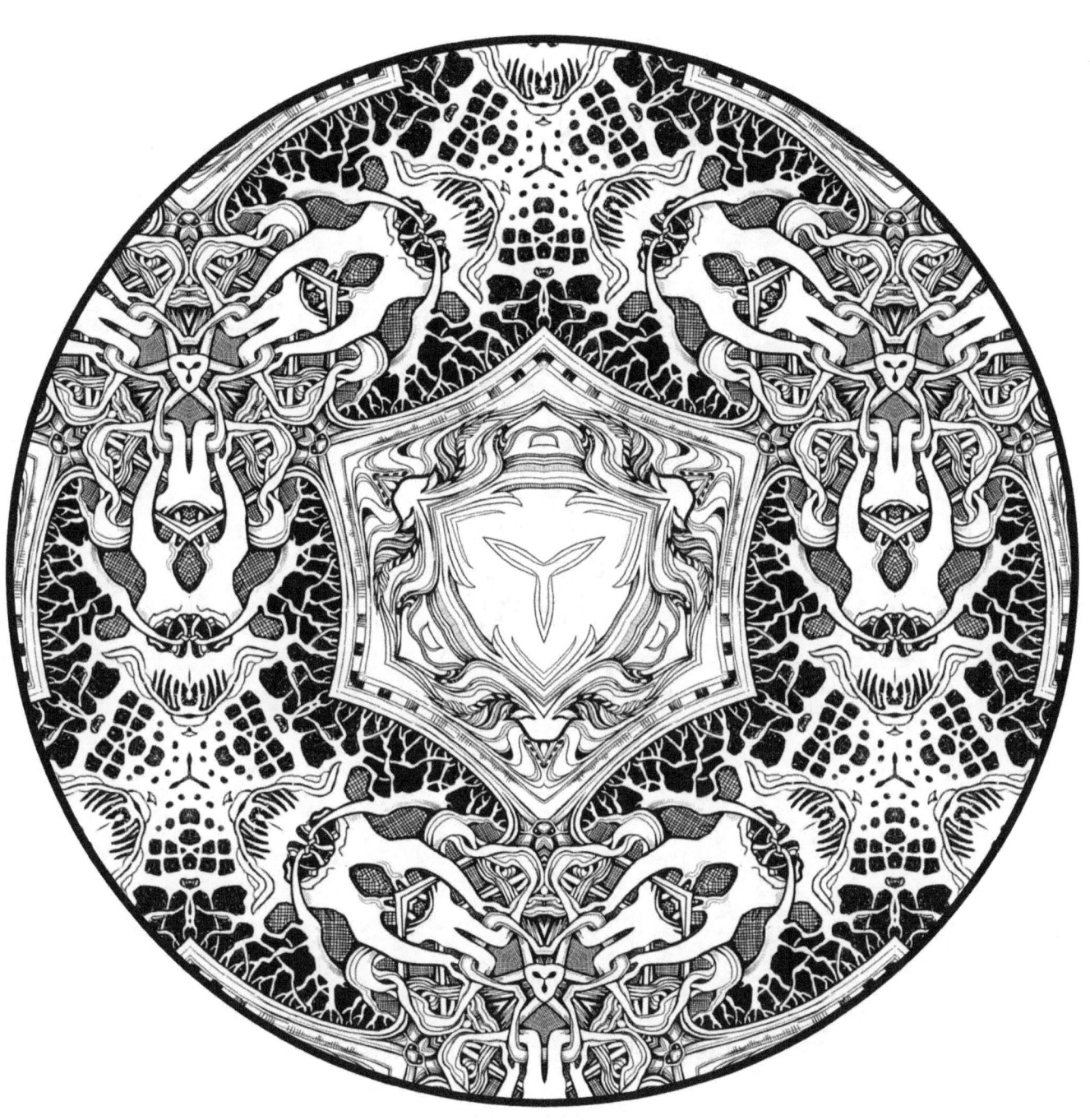

THANK YOU!

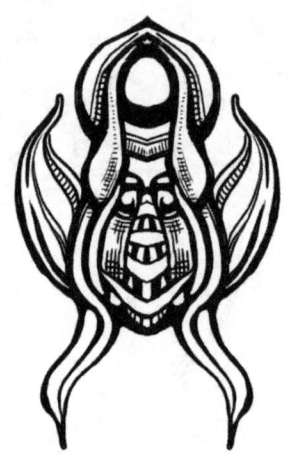

vinnik.net

irinavinnik.com

facebook.com/IrinaVinnikArt

instagram.com/irinavinnik

behance.net/IrinaVinnik